ALLYSON COOPER

Cricut Design Space

Your Specific Guide On Cricut Design Space, To Know At The Best How It Works And Transform Your Project Ideas From Thoughts To Reality

Copyright © 2020 Allyson Cooper

All rights reserved

© **Copyright 2020 - All rights reserved.**

The content contained within this book may not be reproduced, duplicated or transmitted without direct written permission from the author or the publisher.

Under no circumstances will any blame or legal responsibility be held against the publisher, or author, for any damages, reparation, or monetary loss due to the information contained within this book. Either directly or indirectly.

Legal Notice:

This book is copyright protected. This book is only for personal use. You cannot amend, distribute, sell, use, quote or paraphrase any part, or the content within this book, without the consent of the author or publisher.

Disclaimer Notice:

Please note the information contained within this document is for educational and entertainment purposes only. All effort has been executed to present accurate, up to date, and reliable, complete information. No warranties of any kind are declared or implied. Readers acknowledge that the author is not engaging in the rendering of legal, financial, medical or professional advice. The content within this book has been derived from various sources. Please consult a licensed professional before attempting any techniques outlined in this book.

By reading this document, the reader agrees that under no circumstances is the author responsible for any losses, direct or indirect, which are incurred as a result of the use of information contained within this document, including, but not limited to, — errors, omissions, or inaccuracies.

CRICUT DESIGN SPACE

Introduction 5

Chapter 1: The Platform Design Space: Getting Started 11

Chapter 2: Tools And Functions 19

Chapter 3: Projects: How To Start A New Project 42

Chapter 4 Advanced Tips And Techniques 73

Chapter 5 Other Tips & Tricks 92

Chapter 6 Common Problems And How To Solve Them 100

Conclusion 110

CRICUT DESIGN SPACE

Introduction 5

Chapter 1: The Platform Design Space: Getting Started 11

Chapter 2: Tools And Functions 19

Chapter 3: Projects: How To Start A New Project 42

Chapter 4 Advanced Tips And Techniques 73

Chapter 5 Other Tips & Tricks 92

Chapter 6 Common Problems And How To Solve Them 100

Conclusion 110

Introduction

Like many machines that are being placed on the shelves, Cricut also comes with its unique software filled with different settings and features to toggle with. All these components ensure that by using this instrument, it ends up with a beautiful, customized, and accurate product. Cricut's proprietary software is called "Cricut Design Space" and all Cricut devices come with this software, whether it's Cricut mini or Cricut Explore Air. Every Cricut owner must have this software installed on their device and ready to use at any moment. The Cricut must be directly connected to the device via cable or by Bluetooth. Either way, the device needs to be close to the machine. The software is free and has a good user interface that makes it clear and easy to work with, even if you don't have any prior experience with working with a similar device. Its user-friendly feature encourages creativity in an individual. The program is based on Cloud, so even if your device is destroyed or has become inaccessible for any reason, the different design files can be safely recovered. It can be opened onto almost every device, and available at any moment. A laptop, tablet, or mobile can be used as well, and starting a project on one device and switching in between to another is possible. It can even be accessed offline. After the program has been installed, you need to create the designs from the beginning or use any one of thousands of templates already stored in its library. Design Space has a large, diverse collection to push a freshman to start constructing and inventing. One can play around with a variety of fonts, images, and new inspiring ideas. For optimum usage, a Cricut Explorer connected to a computer will be sufficient. This way, all of the features are available, and the machine works without lag.

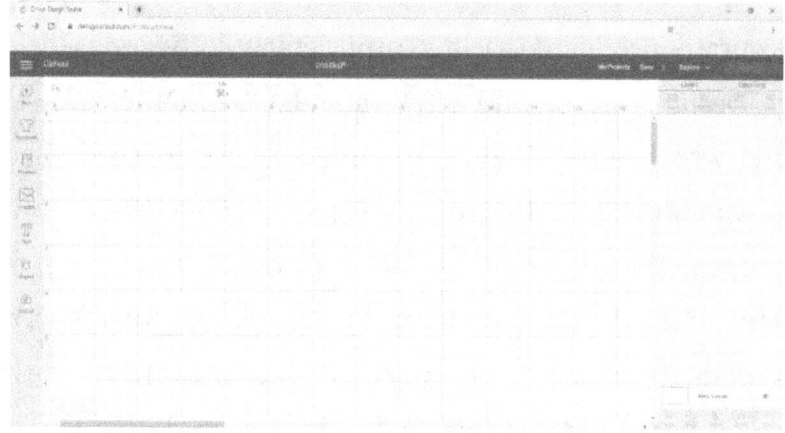

What can I do with it?

Crafting is a hobby that knows no borders, pretty much any shape or design is achieved through this marvelous machine opening to endless uses. For any material needed to be cut, engraved, or etched this machine will fulfill that need. The only boundary would be the lack of one's imagination or capability. From making a few mundane everyday accessories to creating parts for cars, this piece of technology will do the job without fault. Some ideas to use it are as follows:

- For a beginner, it is recommended that they should start working on less complicated projects such as paper crafting. Many people have made a scrapbook in High School, which may or may not be up to the mark, but with this new machine, you can create any papercraft project not only easily but also competently.

- You can use it to make paper pennants to use in a party, or to use it as an accessory to bring to local games and show your support to your team. You can design and shape the flag themselves to give it a hint of uniqueness.

- Cricut can also be used to make greeting cards. Sending your loved ones, a unique and customized card will not only separate you from the crowd but show them that they are special to you. Making greeting cards is very easy even for a beginner by using Cricut.

- The design and uses are not only limited to paper, but you can also make a leather bracelet by using different features in the software provided. Even thick materials and complicated structures cannot hold the Cricut machine back.

- You can make iron-on vinyl T-shirts. Customize T-shirts are usually expensive to order, but you can make them through Cricut easily.

- It can also be used to make new utensils such as customize jars, mugs, plates, etc. You can even make a doormat using this device.

- It can also be used to make home decorations. On holidays you can simply sit at home rather than go out shopping for different decorating items.

- You can make your customized pillows blankets and bed sheets.

- It can also be used for making models of things such as an airplane.

- You can even design beautiful and artful pieces of jewelry.

- Some people use it to make different parts for their cars, motorcycles, etc. if they can't find the right parts anywhere else.

- It can also be used to make banners and signs to attract customers.

The History of Design Space

The first Cricut machine was called the Cricut Personal and was quite a clunky machine. It was heavy, and yet it was smaller than the latest models with a limited cutting space of only 5.5" x 11". It also did not need a computer connected to it to cut, instead, it used cartridges with preloaded images and designs.

The Cricut Personal had a little screen and a lot of buttons. The Cricut Expression 1 was one of the first Cricut cutting machines that could be used both, stand-alone or attached to a computer. It was also the first Cricut machine to have a 12" x 24" cutting ability.

This machine worked with the first version of Cricut software, the predecessor of Design Space, which was known as Cricut Craft Room. As the machines developed so did the Cricut software, with the latest cloud-based system inline according to the newer online trends.

The Cricut Mini was one of the first Cricut cutting machines to rely on a computer to make designs. Up until the introduction of this little crafting machine, the large Cricut cutting machines could use both stand-alone cartridges and Cricut Craft Room. By this time, there was also the Cricut Image Library where Cricut users could download images.

With the launch of the Cricut Explore machine models came Design Space, which eventually took over the roles of both the Cricut Craft Room and Cricut Image Library. The official shutdown of the Cricut Craft Room and Cricut Design Library was announced in 2018.

Since 2018, Cricut Design Space has been greatly improved upon. It is easy to use, and users can upload their images as well as designs. The software is still compatible with the Cricut Cartridges, and Cricut has rolled out a USB cartridge plug for use with machines that no longer have the cartridge slot.

Chapter 1: The Platform Design Space: Getting Started

Setting up your machine could look somehow complicated or tedious. However, this chapter is majorly written to guide you through it, the unboxing process, and the setting up. So, relax and bring that Cricut machine out wherever you've stashed it. It takes approximately 1 hour to finish setting up a Cricut machine. With this guide, you should be done in less than an hour. Let's get right on it, shall we?

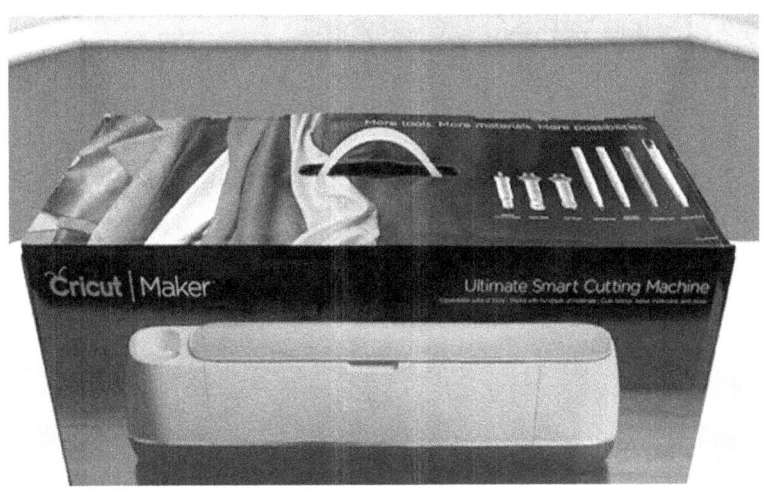

Step 1: Opening the box

To make sure that we are together all the way through, we will go through even the most trivial step; opening the box.

You should have several boxes right now in front of you if you went for the whole Cricut bundle. And there should be a big box among those boxes which contains the Cricut machine itself. If you open that big box, the first thing you should find is a Welcome packet; most of the tools will be in that packet. You should find a welcome manuscript, rotary blade and cover, a USB cable, a fine-point pen, and a packet that contains your first die-cutting project. The USB cable is sometimes the last thing you'll see in this packet, it's probably hidden under every other stuff. Underneath this welcome packet is your Cricut machine.

To find the power cable, you first need to bring out the machine from its box. You will then discover the power cable underneath the box with two cutting mats of standard sizes. That looked easy, right? Let's proceed to the following step.

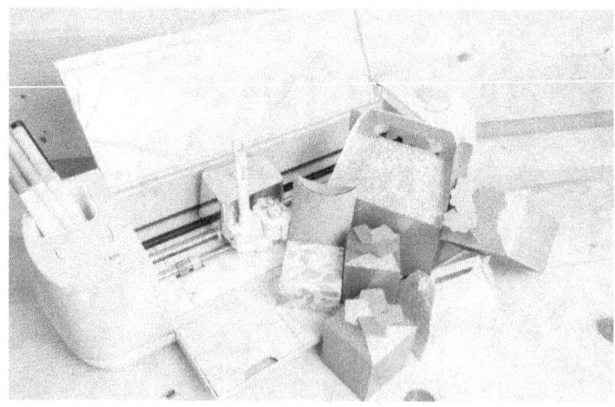

Step 2: Unwrapping your Cricut machine and supplies

We are getting to the exciting part. Let's unwrap your machine and find out what's inside.

When trying to unwrap your machine, you'll find it covered in a protective wrapper that looks filmy and also with a cellophane layer. Try to carefully unwrap the top foam layer so you can see the machine clearly. After that, go on to remove the remaining part of the Styrofoam that protects the inner machine housing.

When you unbox the whole casing, you should expect to find the following tools:

1. Cricut Machine.

2. USB and Power Cables.

3. Rotatory blade with housing.

4. Fine point blade with housing.

5. Fine point pen.

6. Light-Grip and Fabric-Grip Mats (12 x 12).

Step 3: Setting up your machine

Finally, we can move on to getting your machine up and running. Most of what you'll be doing will be technically inclined. You basically need electricity, a mobile phone or computer with internet access. Once you have access to all these, plug your power cord into an electronic outlet, and then switch on your machine.

I'll assume your Cricut machine has Bluetooth function. If it does not have this function, either make use of the USB cable to connect your computer and the Cricut machine or purchase a Bluetooth adapter as soon as you can.

Once they are all connected, open your computer browser to continue the setup. Visit the Cricut Sign-in Page and click on the Sign-in icon. You will have to either sign in with your account details or create a new account for yourself if you don't already have one. This is necessary to access the Cricut Design Space.

If you do not have an active account yet, don't bother to fill in any information on the sign-in fields. Click on the Create Cricut ID in the green box, fill out every field with the required information, and then click on Submit.

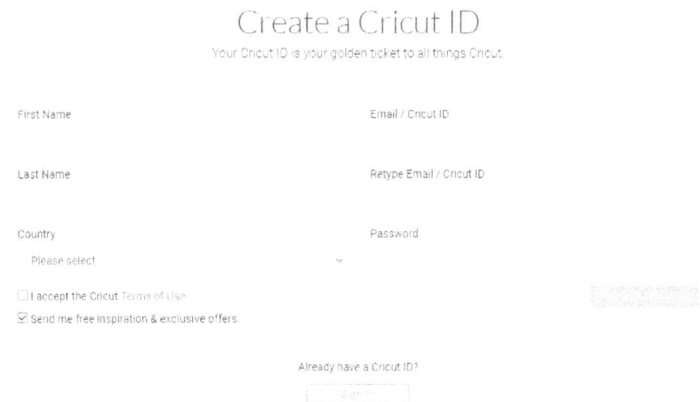

Now, it's time to link your machine to your account. It takes some people a lot of time to finish this part successfully. To make it easier, follow the procedures below:

1. After signing in, go to the upper left corner of the page and click on the drop-down menu icon (with three lines) beside Home.

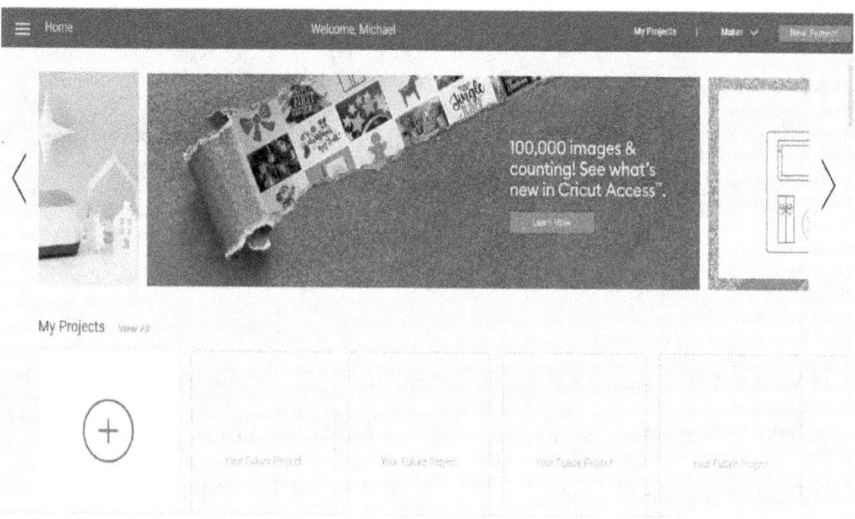

2. When the drop-down menu appears, select the New Machine Setup.

3. On the following screen that pops up, click on your Cricut machine model.

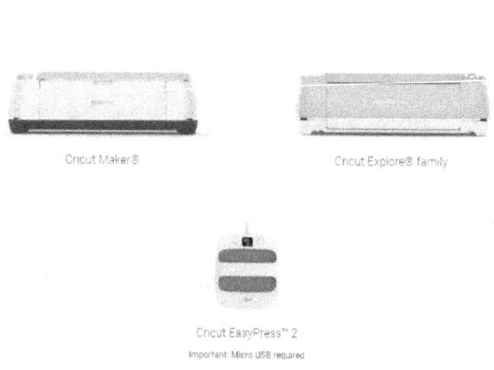

4. Another webpage will appear with instructions on how to connect your machine. Follow the instructions accordingly.

When you follow the instructions, it automatically detects your machine and prompts you to download and install the software.

The site is user-friendly, so you'll be directed on how to go about the installation. And if you already have an account, you may still need to download it again. Cricut updates their design space often, there could be some new tools in the latest version that you don't have access to. It only takes about five minutes to get the installation done.

And there we go; we have concluded the setup procedure on your PC. That wasn't too hard, was it?

You might find the software a little bit complex for you when you first start to explore it. But with constant usage, you'll master it.

Step 4: Claiming your bonus

When you have successfully created an active account on Cricut, you can claim access to Cricut for a whole month for free! It's a welcome bonus from Cricut. You'll have access to different projects, fonts, as well as Cut files. You can exploit this opportunity by making use of the accessible library to work on several fun projects.

Step 5: Commencing your first project

You may want to start practicing with some old projects done by other people or study how they are done before initiate a personal project. Every Cricut machine comes with a trivial project. You'll find it in the welcome pack. You can use this to get familiar with the tools the machine came with.

It may be challenging to make use of the Cricut Design Space without fully knowing its environment. So, stick with small projects till you get better, or ask someone who has more knowledge and experience with Cricut tools to guide you through.

Chapter 2: Tools And Functions

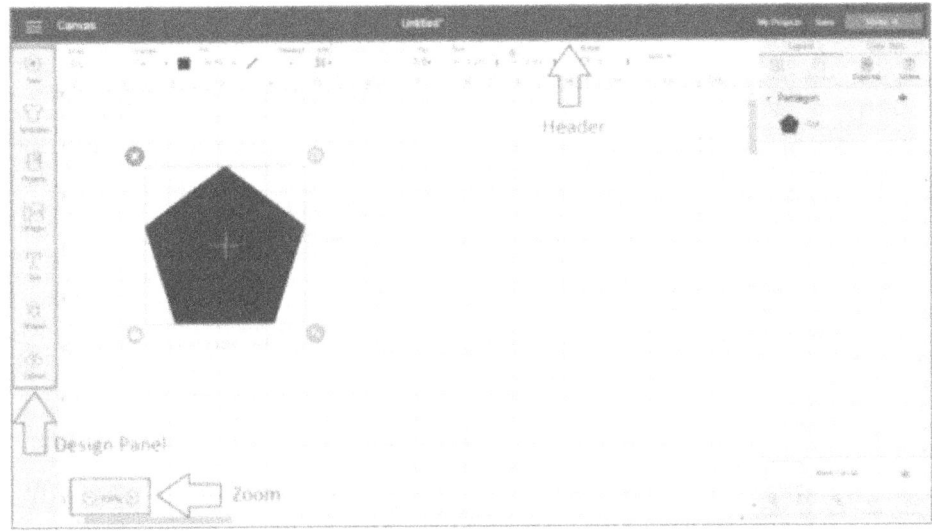

Design Panel

- **New**: To start building a new project you must always click on the 'New' tab.

- **Templates:** To view your final design in the real-life background, you can use any of the relevant templates by clicking on the Template tab.

- **Projects:** To search, select, and cut designs from an already existing project, you can use the Projects tab, which will contain a variety of other projects along with your projects.

- **Images:** The Cricut Image Library contains a wide variety of pictures available at your fingertips for free and to buy. The Images tab will also contain any image that you may upload. So, you can click on the images icon to search, select, and insert any desired image into the Canvas.

- **Text:** You can use the Text tab to add desired phrases or words directly to the Canvas.

- **Shape**: You can use the Shape tab to insert simple shapes square, rectangle, triangle, circle, and score lines into your Canvas.

- **Upload:** You can use the Upload tab to use your image files including jpg, gif, png, bmp, svg, and dxf at no charge.

Header

- **Menu:** The "hamburger" icon on the top left of the screen will allow you to navigate through Cricut Design Space. You can directly access Home, Canvas, and several other Design

Space features, such as New Machine Setup, Settings, Link Cartridges, Help and Sign Out.

- **Page Title:** This will help you remember whether you are on the Home or Canvas page of Design Space. By clicking on the Page Title, you will be able to close an open tab.

- **Project Name:** This will show you the name of your project. If you've not already saved your project, then Untitled will be displayed as the name of the project.

- **My Projects:** You can open your saved projects by clicking on My Projects.

- **Save:** To access your projects across your devices and multiple platforms, you must save your projects to your account by clicking on the Save icon, and providing a name for your projects. Note, if you would like to keep your project private and all to yourself then make sure you uncheck the Public option while saving your project. If you would like to rename your project once has been saved, just click on Save As, and enter a new name for your project.

- **Make it:** Click on the Make it icon when you have prepped your mats and are ready to transfer your project to your Cricut machine.

Zoom

You can Zoom In to look at the finer details of your project, and Zoom Out to see an overview of the same.

The editing panel

The editing panel is at the top of your Canvas Area. It harbors the controls that make it easier for you to work around a project.

The editing panel is divided into two subpanels:

- **Subpanel one:** To allow you to create, name, save, and cut a project.

- **Subpanel two:** To give you all the editing tools.

Subpanel one

The Subpanel one has few icons on it. Let's get the icons explained:

a. **Canvas:** I refer to this as the main button on the design space area. A click on the icon/button and a drop-down menu will appear with a range of options. From the drop-down menu, you can do a lot of settings.

- Home
- Canvas
- New Machine Setup
- Calibration
- Manage Custom Materials
- Update Firmware
- Account Details
- Link Cartridges
- Cricut Access
- Settings
- Legal
- New Features
- United States ▼
- Help
- Sign Out

From this drop-down menu, you can manage your profile. Also, you can calibrate your machine, update firmware, link cartridges, etc. If you have premium access to Cricut Design Space, you can manage your subscription from the drop-down menu. I always advise beginners to take their time and click on all the options on the drop-down menu to understand their functionalities.

b. ***Project name:*** In Cricut Design Space, all new projects are by default Untitled. You can only give a project a name when you have started working on it either by placing an element or a text on it.

c. ***My projects:*** A click on this icon will lead you to all your prior designs if you have any.

d. ***Save:*** This icon becomes functional when you have started working on a project. It is always advisable that you save your project as you design in case of anything going wrong. I learned this the hard way. During my early days with Cricut, I'd only save when I was done with a project until one day, I was about done with a particular project when my browser crashed and that was it with my project. I couldn't recover it because I never save it.

e. ***Maker (Machine):*** This icon has two sub-options when you click on it. The two sub-options include Cricut Maker and Cricut Explore Family. Depending on the machine you are using, you will need to select either of the sub-options while working. These two options have different tools.

f. ***Make it:*** When you are done designing and uploading your projects, this is the final icon you click on to have your project cut.

When you click on Make It, there will be a display on your screen which shows the different colors of your project. From the displayed window you can perform other functions like increasing the number of projects to cut, etc. When you are done with your selection, you can click on Continue to proceed.

Subpanel two (Editing menu)

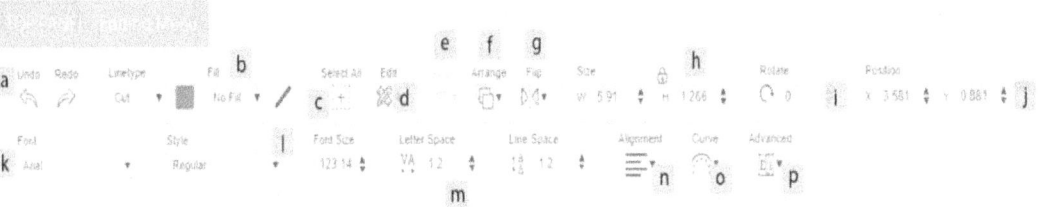

The image above represents the editing panel of the Cricut design space. I will take the icons one after another and explain their functions and usefulness. I lettered the different icons to make it easier for better understanding.

a. ***The Undo and Redo:*** This is a very important icon in your design Canvas. This icon helps you make corrections either by taking you back or forward a bit.

Whenever you are designing, there is possible that you will make mistakes. With the undo and redo option, when you delete something by mistake, clicking redo will bring it back. When you make a mistake in your design space, clicking undo will get out.

b. ***Linetype and Fill:*** The Linetype and Fill icon tells your machine the tools and blades you are going to use for cutting your project.

There are seven options on the Maker Linetype, these include Cut, Draw, Score, Engrave, Deboss, Wave, and Perf.

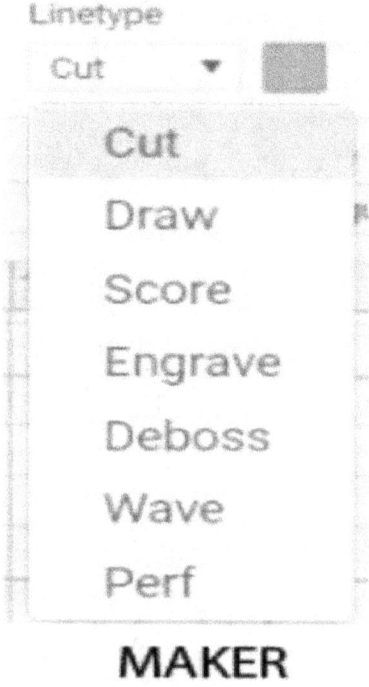

On the Cricut explore family Linetype, there are just three options.

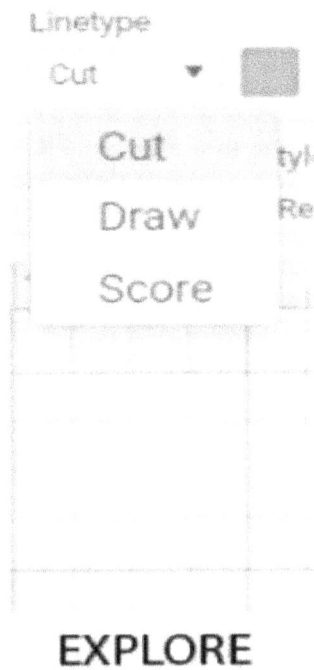

EXPLORE

Explaining the Linetype options tools.

- **Cut:** This is the default line type of all elements on your Canvas, except you upload a png image. When you press 'Make it' at the end of your design, this prompts your machine to cut those designs.

    The Cut option also helps you change the fill of elements in your project. These elements translate into colors of materials that you will use when cutting your project.

- **Draw:** This tool on the linetype helps you write on your design. When you select this option, you will be prompted to choose any of the Cricut pens available for you. Upon selection of a particular pen, the layers on your Canvas area will be listed with the color of the pen you picked. When the Draw tool is selected and you click on Make it, your Cricut will either write or draw instead of cutting. Also, this option doesn't color your designs at all.

- ***Score:*** The Score tool is an important version of the scoring line which is located on the left panel of your Canvas space. When this tool is selected and assigned to a layer, all the designs will appear dashed or scored.

  At the end of your project when you click on Make it, your Cricut will score the materials instead of cutting them.

- ***Engrave, wave, deboss, and perf:*** These are new tools added by Cricut to the Cricut Maker Machine. With these tools, you will be able to create amazing designs of different materials. They are still pretty new, so try them out when you can.

  One thing I know for sure about these tools is that they work with the Quick Swap Adaptive Tool.

The Fill tool

This option/tool is used mainly for patterns and printing. The Fill option gets activated only when you are using Cut as a linetype. When you have No Fill it means that you won't be printing any project.

The Print tool is the most important tool on your design Canvas because it makes it possible for you to print your projects and cut them.

When the Fill tool is active, when you click Make it, firstly, the files will be sent to your printer while your Cricut does all the cutting.

The Print type has two sub-options that allows you to perform magic on your Canvas. These options include Color and Pattern. When you explore these options you will be amazed at the project you will create

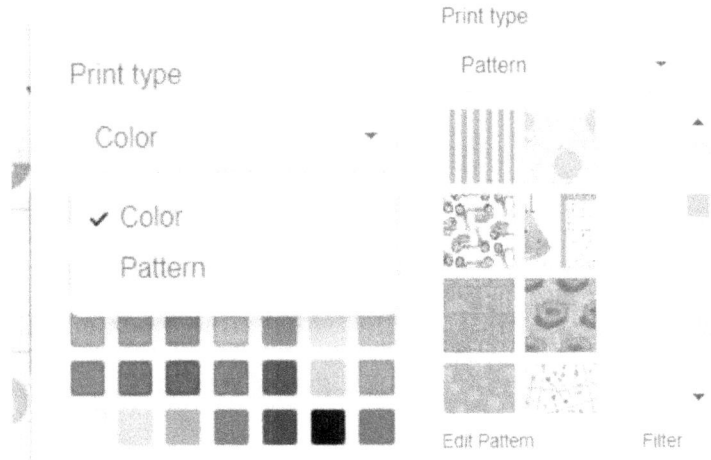

c. ***Select all:*** This tool serves to help you select all the elements in your Canvas area. Sometimes it is a hassle to select elements individually, so this tool helps you make multiple selections at the same time.

d. **Edit:** The Edit icon when clicked on has three tools, Cut, Copy, and Paste. With these options, you can copy an element, paste a copied element, or cut off an unwanted element on your Canvas.

Once you have made a selection on your Canvas, the Cut and Copy tools get activated. When you have copied or cut an element, the Paste option gets activated.

e. **The Align icon:** If you have ever used another design tool, this will be an easy walk around for you. But if you have not, it's easy to get a hang of.

The Alignment icon is one you should master as it is very important while working on your project. The Alignment tool helps your project stay perfectly organized and on the same line.

The Align icon has a drop-down menu that contains other alignment tools.

Let's take a look at the functions on the Align drop-down menu.

Align: This particular tool allows you to align all the elements in your design. It is activated when you select two or more elements on your Canvas.

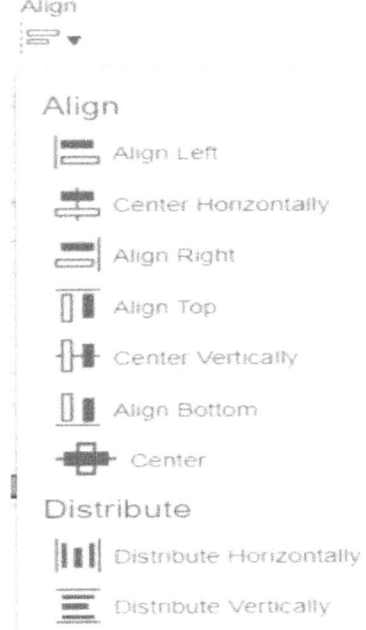

- o *Align Left:* This function takes all the selected elements and aligns them to the left. Whichever element that is furthest at the left determines the alignment.

- *Center Horizontal:* Just like every other alignment option, this will align all the elements on your project horizontally, while the texts and images are centered.

- *Alight Right:* When you activate this option, all the elements on your project will be aligned to the right. Whichever element that is furthest at the right determines the alignment.

- *Alight Top:* This option aligns all the elements of your project to the top. Whichever element that is furthest at the top determines the alignment.

- *Center Vertically:* With this option, all the elements of your project will be aligned to the center. When working with columns and you want them organized and properly aligned, use this option.

- *Align Bottom:* This alignment option will align all the selected elements on your project to the bottom. Whichever element that is furthest at the bottom determines the alignment.

- *Center:* When this option is clicked on, it perfectly centers every element on your project: shapes, text, images.

- *Distribute:* The distribute option gives equal spacing to all the elements on your project. In Cricut Design Space, there is nothing as time-consuming as trying to manually allocate equal space between the elements on your project so, with this tool, all your problems are solved. For this tool to be activated, two or more elements must be selected on your project.

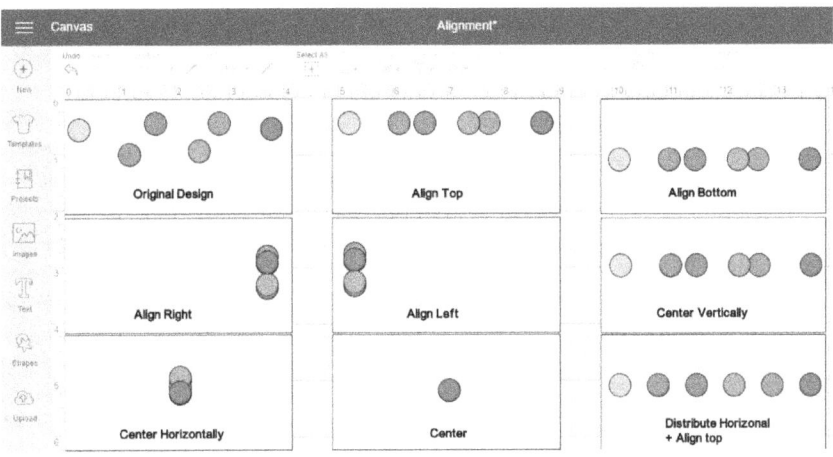

- o *Distribute Horizontally:* This option will distribute the elements on your project horizontally. The furthest elements left and right on your project will determine the length of the distribution.

- o *Distribute Vertically:* This option will distribute the elements on your project vertically. The furthest elements top and bottom on your project will determine the length of the distribution.

f. **Arrange:** The Arrange option helps put the elements on your project in the right place. When you are working on a project with multiple text, images, and designs, there is every probability that the new elements you add will be placed in front of others, but, in an actual sense, you want them placed at the back. The arrange option makes it easier to do that.

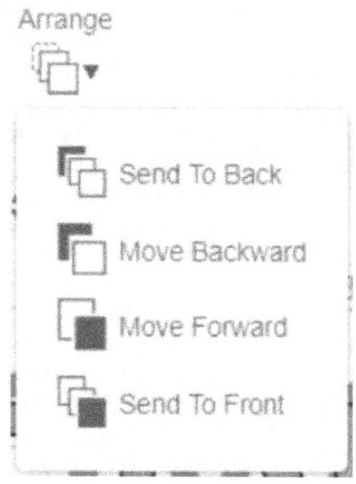

The Arrange option has other sub-options which includes:

- *Send Back:* This action will move all selected elements on your project to the back.

- *Move Backward:* This action will move all selected elements on your project one step back. This simply means that activating this item will just take the element(s) only one step back instead of all the way back behind other elements.

- *Move Forward:* This action will move the selected element(s) a step forward.

- *Send to Front:* This action will move the selected element(s) to the front of every other element on the project.

g. **Flip:** The Flip icon gives you the ability to reflect your designs on your Cricut Canvas.

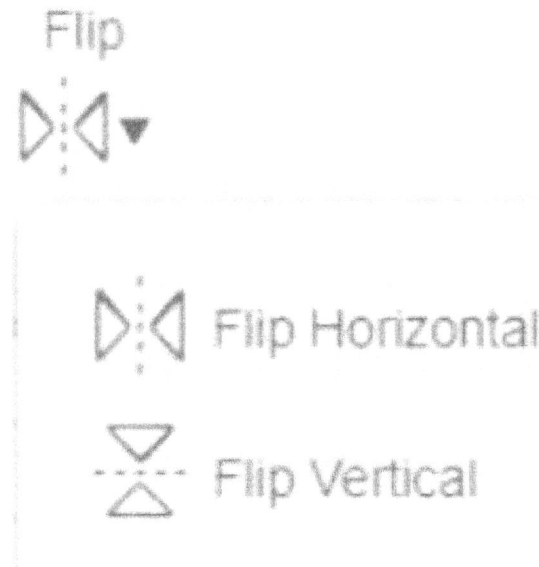

The Flip option has two sub-options:

- *Flip Horizontal:* This action when activated reflects the images on your design horizontally. The best way I can explain is that Flip horizontally helps you duplicate a design. When you have a design at the right and want to duplicate the same design at the left, Flip horizontally helps you to do that.

- *Flip Vertical:* This action perfectly helps you create a shadow effect on your design by duplicating the selected design vertically.

h. **Size:** Every element you introduce to your design Canvas (text, image, shape) has a size. Sometimes you may not want to alter the size, but the Size icon gives you the ability to modify elements to any size of your choice.

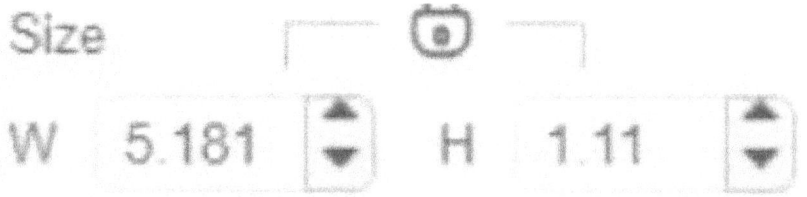

After modifying the size of an image, it is essential to click the lock icon on the size option. This is the way to tell your Cricut program that you don't want to keep those same dimensions as default.

i. **Rotate:** The rotate action helps you rotate an element to the desired angle. It can get tedious trying to get an image on your project to the right angle manually, but with the rotate option, it is very easy.

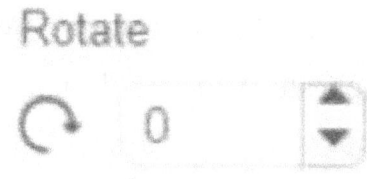

j. **Position:** This option shows you exactly where your elements are on a design Canvas area. With this tool, you can move elements on your project around by specifying where you want them to be.

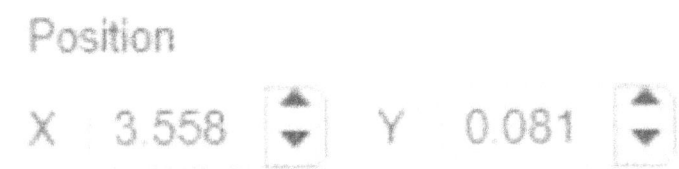

This is pretty much an advanced tool, but a similar option to this is the alignment tool.

k. **Font:** This option gives you access to the different text fonts available for your design on Cricut. You can choose any font of your choice to work with.

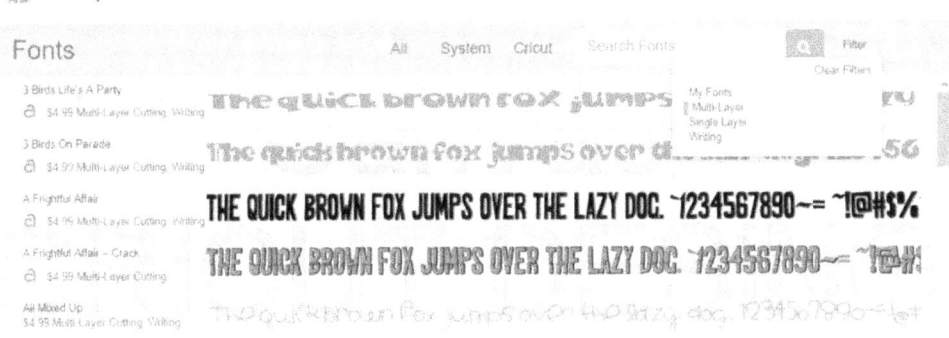

1. ***Style:*** The Style option works in hand with Fonts. Once you select a font of your choice, the next step is to choose the style. The style option has some sub-options.

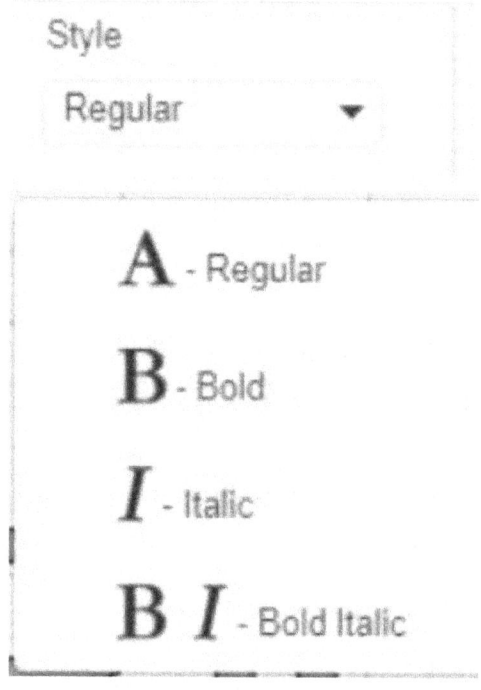

The Regular is the default style of your design Canvas. Bold makes your chosen font appear thicker. Italic makes your chosen font tilt to the right, while Bold Italic makes the italic font thicker.

m. ***Font Size, Letter Space, and Line Space:*** These three options are very amazing as it brings a sort of perfection to your projects.

```
Font Size            Letter Space           Line Space
60.1      ▲          VA    1.2    ▲         ↕A   1.2    ▲
          ▼                       ▼              A     ▼
```

- *Font size:* You can change the size of your text in the Font Size area.

- *Letter space:* While some fonts have considerable space between the letters others don't really have. The letter space option allows you to manage the spacing between letters.

- *Line space:* This option allows you to manage the space between the text lines in a paragraph.

n. ***Alignment:*** Don't get confused, this particular alignment is different from the other alignment explained initially. These alignment options work with paragraphs.

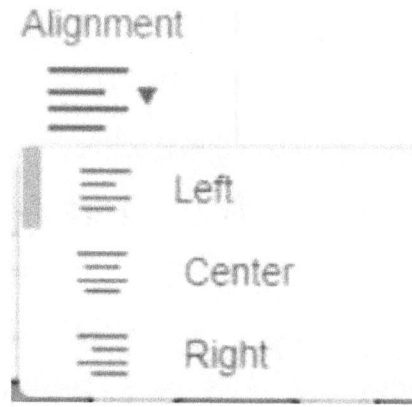

The Alignment option has other sub-options:

- *Left:* This action aligns selected paragraph(s) to the left.

- *Center:* This action aligns selected paragraph(s) to the center.

- *Right:* This action aligns selected paragraph(s) to the right.

o. ***Curve:*** Do you want to make your text shaped? This option is your best bet. The Curve option allows you to make your texts curved.

By moving the slider right or left it curves your texts upward or inward.

p. ***Advance:*** Don't get scared about this option, it is as easy as other options. Even though as a beginner you may not use it often, but once you get a hang of it you are good to go.

Chapter 3: Projects: How To Start A New Project

Starting a New Project - The Basics

When you are starting a new project, you'll want to know what that project will be, and what materials you will be using before doing anything else.

For example, if you want to cut vinyl letters to place on wood, you'll need to know all dimensions, so your letters fit evenly and centered on the wood. You'll need wood that vinyl can adhere to without the risk of peeling. And you'll want to be sure that your wood is sanded and finished according to your desire because you don't want any imperfections. You may find even with store-bought wood pieces advertised as ready-to-use, there are tiny imperfections.

You want to make sure when working with fabric that you know what inks or vinyl will adhere to the surface. You don't want any peeling or cracking to happen to your beautiful design.

When working with any kind of fabric, including Canvas bags, you'll want to pre-wash for sizing because shrinkage, after your design has been set, can cause the design to become distorted.

If you aren't sure exactly what you want to do, have something in mind so that you aren't wasting a lot of materials by trial and error. The cost of crafting materials can increase, so you'll want to eliminate as much potential waste as possible.

If you're new to Cricut Design Space, start with something simple. You don't want to get in over your head. That's the worst thing you can do when you learn any new craft. There are many used Cricut machines for sale, and while some users sell because they upgraded, others are users who gave up. You made the investment and you'll want to get a return on that investment.

Ready to conquer Cricut Design Space?

To keep up with any changes, you should subscribe to the company email list or check the Cricut website often.

Let's begin by clicking on New from our menu options. It's at the very top of the Canvas in the left corner.

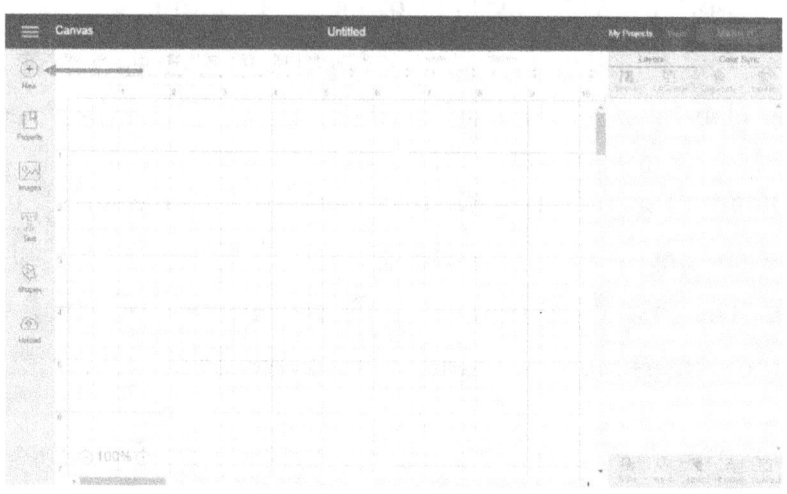

An empty Canvas will appear. You might have previously started a project, and in that case, the machine will detect it in the queue, and you'll be asked if you want to replace the project. If you don't want to replace it, be sure you save all of your changes or you might lose them, and you don't want to lose all of your hard work. It's important to not rush so that you don't accidentally delete a project you want to be saved. When you've completed that action, you'll be returned to your new blank Canvas.

First, you want to name your project. Use a name that closely relates to it so you aren't getting projects confused. If you have a lot of projects, and you don't use a system to identify them, you might want to consider it.

As you can see from our illustration, everything you need is on the left, under the 'New' icon.

Different templates appear by clicking on the templates icon, however, these are only to get an idea of how your final project will look.

- Projects allow you to access the Make It Now™ platform. There are so many to choose from and you might find yourself spending a lot of time looking at them all.

- Images are just what they say. This is the icon you need to add an image or images to your project.

- Text is for writing the text if your project has words.

- Shapes allow you to add different shapes such as circles, squares, and hearts.

- Upload your images and/or begin cutting. This is the final design step!

If you know what your project is going to be, you can go to the Projects icon and begin to customize it or start cutting.

We have talked about subscriptions, and it should be noted that you can purchase a one-time design for a nominal fee. You can also purchase designs from Etsy and other craft sites.

When you've done your design, don't forget to save it. You will get the option of Save or Save as. You will get a message letting you know that your project was successfully saved. Save as will save your project as a new one and keep the old one under its name. You could need to rename your project with the Save as a feature.

It's easy to get so caught up in the design process and anxious to see the finished project that we can forget to hit Save. Your project should automatically save in the cloud, but if it doesn't, you'll have it. It's always better to be safe than sorry.

Now, you've brought your design to your screen. You want to give it a final look and make certain everything is where you want it. If you're ready to cut, click Make It.

If your Cricut machine isn't turned on do it now, and have all your materials ready. You'll want to follow the prompts. Set your material and load your tools and mat. Press the Go icon and wait. When the cutting is done, press Unload and carefully remove the mat.

Voila! Your project is finished. Wasn't that easy?

Basic Object Editing

The Canvas comes equipped with an editing toolbar that allows you to make corrections.

If you make a mistake, you can easily fix it. You can use the Undo and Redo buttons by clicking them the required number of times.

The Undo icon will let you get rid of something you don't like. It acts as an eraser, and each click will undo the previous action.

If you accidentally delete something, you can use the Redo button. This will restore your work.

Another editing tool is the linetype dropdown that will let you change to a Cut, Draw or Score object. It communicates with your machine so it knows what tools you're going to be using.

Cut is the default linetype you'll use unless you've uploaded a jpeg or png image. When you click on the "make it" icon, those designs will be cut.

Use Draw if you want to write on your design. You'll be prompted to select a pen, and you'll use this to write or draw.

Tip: This option won't color your designs.

You can use the Score feature to score or dash your design.

The Edit icon lets you Cut, Copy, and Paste from the Canvas. It functions with a drop-down menu and you use it by selecting the elements you want to edit from your Canvas.

The program also features an Align tool that will let you move your design around on the Canvas. If you've used a design program before, this should be easy for you to do. If you haven't, it can be tricky.

Functions of the alignment tool

The following are the functions you can use to move your design on the Canvas. You might want to practice using these until you're comfortable with them.

Align allows you to align all of your designs by selecting two or more elements on your Canvas.

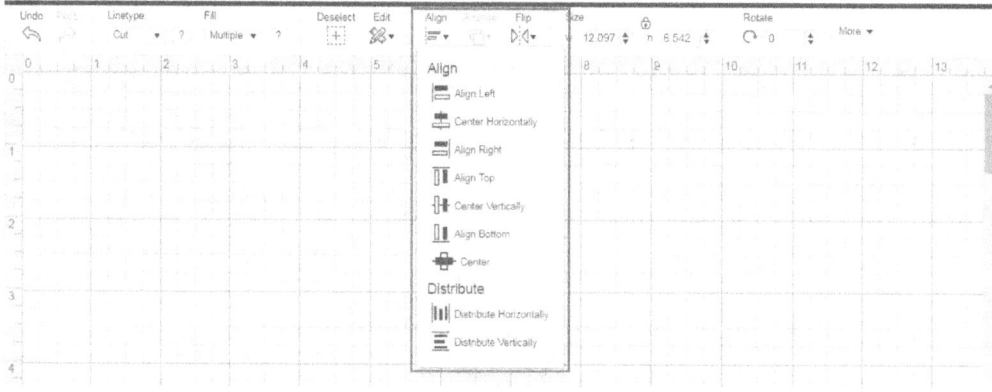

- Align Left will move everything to the left.

- Center Horizontal will align horizontally and will center text and images. This brings everything to the center.

- Align Right will move everything to the right.

- Align Top will move the designs you select to the top of the Canvas.

- Center vertically will align your selections vertically.

- Align Bottom will bring your selections to the bottom.

- Center will bring everything to the center, vertically and horizontally.

You can also distribute vertically and horizontally. This will give you some space between your design elements.

You can also flip, arrange, rotate, and size your design. All of these features are handy, and once you master them you can quickly align your design to your preference.

Using images in the design space

For starters, the Cricut Design Space library has over 60,000 images available for crafters to use in their crafts. Every update of Cricut brings about newly added images, so really, you are well equipped.

Selecting images for your project

As always, everything begins in your Design Space. Here, select New Project and then click on the Images tool located in your design panel. It will open up the images library to search for any image you want—either scroll or search for a specific image using the search bar.

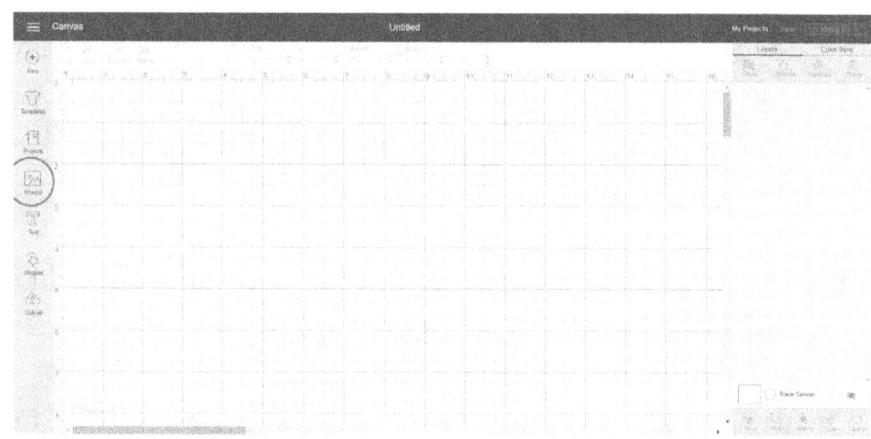

Search using category

To make your search a lot easier, you can also search by using the Category function. Search for images using the Free this Week, Most Popular, and Recently Added options.

As you scroll down, you can also see the list of categories that are listed alphabetically. So essentially, you have plenty of different ways and options to find the perfect image for your design.

Search using cartridge

Before the latest updates came in, crafters using Cricut Design Space and Cricut Craft Room software could remember the physical cartridge to use with the Cricut machine. But now, you can do this via the Design Space. Practically, the Cartridge images arrange by theme, so this is another excellent way to find ideas for your project. If needed, you can also buy the entire cartridge, which is usually cheaper than buying a single image. Of course, this option makes sense only if you use the Cricut often, and you've explored all of those images on the Design Space and can't find what you want.

Filter your image search results

You can always use the Filter option only to show My Images, Uploaded, Free, Cricut Access, or Purchased at any point in your image search process. If you are not familiar with Cricut, you can easily find free images that allow you to test and try to design spaces before delving into buying prints.

About the images

As you go through your Design Space, you will see some images that have the Cricut Access symbol. It's usually a little green flag icon with an A on it. The images and fonts with this symbol are available only if you have subscribed to the Access subscriptions.

Suppose you are a heavy Cricut user, and you've explored all the images on the Library, or the photos on the Library are not according to your likeness or taste.

The other thing you want to know about the Images Library is the little italicized I on the right-hand corner for some images. After clicking it, you will see the image name, number, and the cartridge it belongs to. You can click on the link of the cartridge to see all images contained in the cartridge.

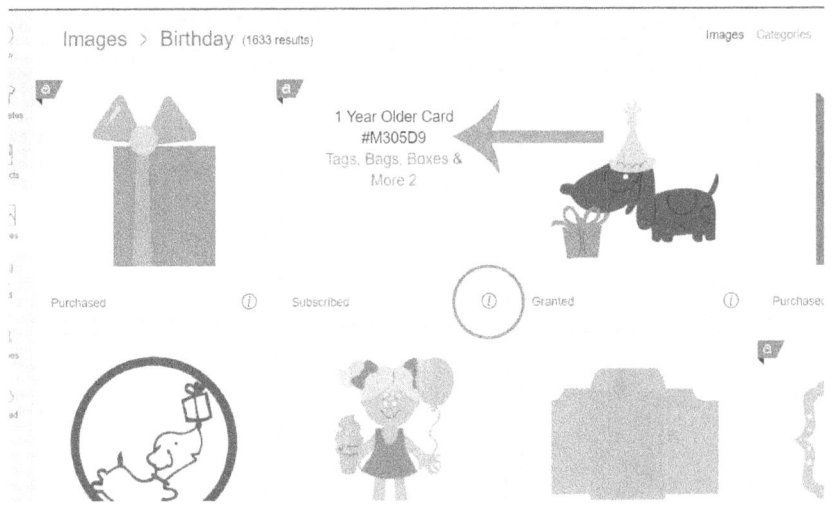

You would also see a printer icon on some of these images. It would mean that they design for ready-to-go use.

Adding images to your project

To select one or more images for your project, just click on each image. All you need to do is choose the photos you want, as many as you would like, and then click on Insert Images to include your Design Space images.

When the images are on your blank Canvas on Design Space, you can resize them or edit them according to how you want them on the design.

For any image that you select, there will be a box around it. You will see a red X mark in the upper left corner for you to delete the image. You can also rotate the image or even adjust the painting size according to your liking. You can also lock or unlock the image proportions. If you want to delete a photo, you no longer wish to work, just select the image, click the red X in the left top corner, select the image in the layers panel, and click the Delete button.

Searching and adding images for your project is extremely easy with the Design Space. Before you subscribe to the Access or getting a Cartridge, explore what Cricut has to offer first because with 60,000 over images you are bound to find something you like to do a beautiful project.

Project ideas to try

With Cricut, the ideas for projects are so vast, you'll be amazed at how much you can do. So, what are some ideas that could work for you? Here are a few that you can consider, and some of the best project ideas for those who are stumped on where to begin!

Easy Projects

Custom Shirts

Custom shirts are incredibly easy. The beauty of this is, you can use the Cricut fonts or system options, and from there, you can simply print it on. Personally, I like to use the iron-on vinyl, because it's easy to work with. Just take your image and upload it into Design Space. Then, go to the Canvas and find the image you want. Once you've selected the image, you click on the whitespace that will be cut– remember to get the insides, too. Make sure that you choose cut image, not print from cut image, and then place it on the Canvas to the size of your liking. Put the iron-on vinyl shiny side down, turn it on, and then select iron-on from the menu. Choose to cut, and make sure you mirror the image. Once done, pull off the extra vinyl to remove the vinyl between the letters. There you go! A simple shirt.

Vinyl Decals

Vinyl can also be used to make personalized items, such as water bottle decals. First, design the text– you can pretty much use whatever you want for this. From here, create a second box and make an initial, or whatever design you want. Make sure that you resize this to fit the water bottle, as well.

From here, load your vinyl, and make sure that you use transfer tape on the vinyl itself once you cut it out. Finally, when you adhere the lettering to the bottle, go from the center and then push outwards, smoothing as you go. It takes a bit, but there you have it–simple water bottles that children will love! This is a wonderful, simple project for those of us who aren't really that artistically inclined but want to get used to making Cricut items.

Printable Stickers

Printable stickers are the next project. This is super simple and fun for parents and kids. For this project, the Explore Air 2 machine works best.

With this one, you want the Print then cut feature, since it makes it much easier. To begin, go to Design Space and download images of ice cream or whatever you want, or upload images of your own. You click on a New Project, and on the left side that says Images, you can choose the ones you like, and insert more of these on there.

From here, choose the image and flatten it, since this will make it into one piece rather than just a separate file for each. Resize as needed to make sure that they fit where you're putting them.

You can copy and paste each element until you're done. Once ready, press Save, and then choose this as a Print then cut image. Click the big button at the bottom that says make it. Make sure everything is good, then press continue, and from there, you can load the sticker paper into the machine. Make sure to adjust this to the right setting, which for sticker paper is the vinyl set. Put the paper into there and load them in, and when ready, the press goes – it will then cut the stickers as needed.

From there, take them out and decorate. You can use ice cream or whatever sticker image you want!

Personalized Pillows

Personalized pillows are another fun idea, and are incredibly easy to make. To begin, you open up Design Space and choose a New Project. From here, select the icon at the bottom of the screen itself, choosing your font. Type the words you want, and drag the text as needed to make it bigger.

You can also upload images, too, if you want to create a huge picture on the pillow itself.

From here, you want to press the Attach button for each box, so that they work together and both are figured when centered, as well.

Then you press Make it – and you want to turn to mirror on, since this will be, again, on iron-on vinyl. From here, you load the iron-on vinyl with the shiny side down, the press continues, follow the prompts, and make sure it's not jammed in, either.

Let the machine work its magic with cutting and from there, you can press the weeding tool to get the middle areas out.

Set your temperature on the easy press for the right settings, and then push it onto the material, ironing it on and letting it sit for 10 to 15 seconds. Let it cool, and then take the transfer sheet off.

There you have it! A simple pillow that works wonders for your crafting needs.

Cards

Finally, cards are a great project idea for Cricut makers. They're simple, and you can do the entire project with cardstock.

To make this, you first want to open up Design Space, and from there, put your design in. If you like images of ice cream, then use that. If you want to make Christmas cards, you can do that, too. Basically, you can design whatever you want to on this.

Now, you'll then want to add the text. You can choose the font that you want to use, and from there, write out the message on the card, such as "Merry Christmas." At this point, instead of choosing to cut, you want to choose the right option–the 'Make it' option. You don't have to mirror this, but check that your design fits properly on the cardstock itself. When choosing material for writing, make sure you choose the cardstock.

From there, insert your cardstock into the machine, and then, when ready, you can press Go and the Cricut machine will make your card. This may take a minute, but once it's done, you'll have a wonderful card in place. It's super easy to use.

Cricut cards are a great personalized way to express yourself, creating a one-of-a-kind, sentimental piece for you to gift to friends and family.

Medium Projects

Cricut cake toppers

Cricut cake toppers have a little bit of added difficulty because they require some precise scoring. The Cricut maker is probably the best piece of equipment for the job, and here, we'll tell you how to do it. The scoring tool is your best bet since this will make different shapes even easier, as well. You will want to make sure you have cardstock and the cutting mat, along with a fine-point blade for cutting. The tape is also handy for these.

First, go to Design Space and choose the rosettes you want. From there, press 'Make it' and follow the prompts. It will then ask you whether you want the single or double wheel. Scoring shells are meant to create extra-deep score lines in materials, to get the perfect fold. The single wheel will make one crease, and the double wheel will make a parallel wheel that will crease—perfect for specialty items. Plus, the double wheel is thicker, so it's easier to fold.

Once you score everything, you remove it and replace the scoring wheel with the fine-point blade.

From here, you simply fold everything and just follow the line. This should make the rosette, and you can then use contrasting centers and create many of these to form a nice backdrop.

Cricut gift bags

Next are gift bags. Remember to put the foil poster board face-down on the mat itself, to help prevent the material from cracking and showing through to the white backdrop, when you fold them together after you score them.

To make these, you want to implement the template that you'd like to use in Design Space. From here, I do suggest cutting out the initial design first, and then putting it back in to create scoring lines, following the same steps. After that, you can take your item and fold along the score lines, and then use adhesive or glue to help put it all together. This is a great personalized way to do it, but it can be a bit complicated to work with at first.

Cricut fabric coasters

Fabric coasters with a Cricut maker are great, and they need only a few supplies. These include the maker itself, cotton fabric, fusible fleece, a rotary cutting mat or some scissors, a sewing machine, and an iron.

Cut the fabric to about 12 inches to fit the cutting mat – if it's longer, you can hang it off, just be careful.

From here, go to Design Space, then click shapes and make a heart. You can do this with other shapes, too. Resize it to about 5 inches wide. Press Make it, and you'll want to make sure you create four copies. Press continue, and then choose medium fabrics similar to cotton. Load the mat and cut, and then you do it again with the fusible fleece on the cutting mat, changing it to 4.75 inches. This time, when choosing the material, go to more, and select fusible fleece. Cut the fusible fleece, and attach these to the back of the heart with the iron and repeat with the second.

Sew the two shapes together, leaving a gap for stitching and turning. Clip the curves, turn it inside out, and then fold in the edges and stitch it.

There you go–a fusible fleece heart coaster. It's a little bit more complicated, but it's worth trying out.

Difficult Projects

Giant Vinyl Stencils

Vinyl stencils are a good thing to create too, but they can be hard. Big vinyl stencils are an excellent Cricut project, and you can use them in various places, including bedrooms for kids.

You only need the Explore Air 2, the vinyl that works for it, a pallet, sander, and, of course, paint and brushes. The first step is preparing the pallet for painting, or whatever surface you plan on using this for.

From here, you create the mermaid tail (or any other large image) in Design Space. Now, you'll learn immediately that big pieces are hard to cut and impossible to do all at once in Design Space.

What you do is to section each design accordingly, and remove any middle pieces. Next, you can add square shapes to the image, slicing it into pieces so that it can be cut on a cutting mat that fits.

At this point, you cut out the design by pressing Make it, choosing your material, and working in sections.

From here, you put it on the surface that you're using, piecing this together with each line, and you should have one image after piecing it all together. Then, draw out the line on vinyl and paint the initial design. For the second set of stencils, you can simply trace the first one and then paint the inside of them. At this point, you should have the design finished. When done, remove it very carefully.

And there you have it! Bigger stencils can be a bit of a project since it involves trying to use multiple designs all at once, but with the right care and the right designs, you'll be able to create whatever it is you need to in Design Space so you can get the results you're looking for.

Cricut quilts

Quilts are a bit hard to do for many people, but did you know that you can use Cricut to make it easier? Here, you'll learn an awesome project that will help you do this. To begin, you start with the Cricut Design Space. Here, you can add different designs that work for your project. For example, if you're making a baby blanket or quilt with animals on it, you can add little fonts with the names of the animals, or different pictures of them, too. From here, you want to make sure you choose the option to reverse the design. That way, you'll have it printed on correctly. At this point, make your quilt. Do various designs and sew the quilt as you want to.

From here, you should cut it on the iron-on heat transfer vinyl. You can choose that, and press Cut. The image will then cut into the piece.

At this point, it'll cut itself out, and you can proceed to transfer this with some parchment paper. Use an EasyPress for best results and push it down. There you go, an easy addition that will definitely enhance the way your blankets look.

Step-by-step guide on some Cricut projects

Felt roses

Materials needed

- SVG files with 3D flower design.

- Felt sheets.

- Fabric grip mat.

- Glue gun.

Steps

1. First of all, upload your flower SVG graphics into the Cricut design.

2. Having placed the image in the project, select it, right-click, and click Ungroup. This allows you to resize each flower independently of the others. Since you are using felt, it is recommended that each of the flowers is at least 6 inches in size.

3. Create several copies of the flowers, as many as you wish, selecting the colors you want in the Color Sync Panel (by dragging and dropping the images on to the color you would want them to be cut on). Immediately you're through with that, click on Make it on the Cricut Design Space.

4. Click on Continue. After your Cricut Maker is connected and registered, under the Materials options, select Felt.

5. If your rotary blade is not in the machine, insert it. Next, on the Fabric Grip Mat, place the first felt sheet (in order of color), then, load them into your Cricut Maker. Press the Cut button when this is done.

6. After they are cut, begin to roll the cut flowers one by one. Do this from the outside in. Make sure that you do not roll them too tight. Use the picture as a guide.

7. Apply hot glue on the circle right in the middle and press the felt flowers that you rolled up on the glue. Hold this in place and do not let it go until the glue binds it.

8. Wait for the glue to dry, and your roses are ready for use.

Custom coasters

Materials needed:

- Free pattern templates.

- Monogram design (in Design Space).

- Cardstock or printing paper.

- Butcher paper.

- Lint-free towel.

- Round coaster blanks.

- Light grip mat.

- Easy Press 2 (6″ x 7″ recommended).

- Easy Press mat.

- Infusible ink pens.

- Heat resistant tape.

- Cricut bright pad (optional) for easier tracing.

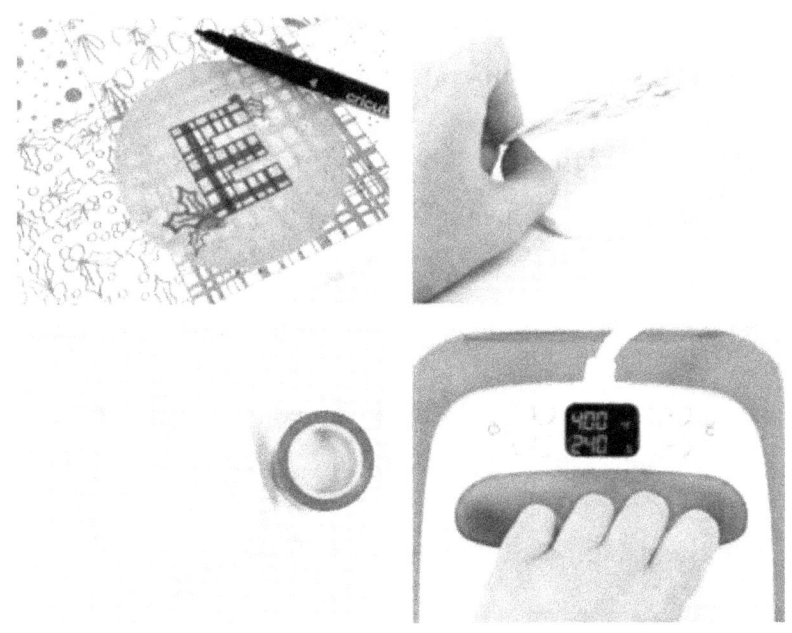

Steps

1. In Cricut Design Space, open the monogram design. You can click Customize and choose the designs that you want to cut out or just go ahead and cut out all the letters.

2. Click on Make It.

3. On the page displayed, click on Mirror Image to make the image mirrored. This must be done whenever you are using infusible ink. For your material, choose Cardstock. Place your cardstock on the mat and load it into the machine; then press the Cut button on the Cricut machine.

4. After the Cricut machine is done cutting, unload it, and remove the done monograms from the mat.

5. Trace the designs onto the cut-out. If you have a Cricut Bright Pad, you can use it to carry out this step much more easily, as it will make the trace lines easier to identify. Tracing should be done using Cricut infusible ink pens.

6. Use the lint-free towel to wipe the coaster. Ensure that no residue is left behind to prevent any marks left on the blank.

7. Make the design centered on the face down coaster.

8. Get a piece of butcher paper which is about an inch larger on each side of the coaster and place on top of the design.

9. Tape this butcher paper onto the coaster using heat resistant tape, to hold the design fast.

10. Set the temperature of your Easy Press to 400 degrees and set the timer to 240 seconds.

11. Place another butcher paper piece on your Easy Press mat, set the coaster on top of it, face up.

12. Place another piece of butcher paper on top of these. Place the already preheated Easy Press on top of the coaster and start the timer.

13. Lightly hold the Easy Press in place (without moving) or leave it in place right on the coaster –if on a perfectly flat surface–till the timer goes off.

14. After this is done, gently remove the second Easy Press, then turn it off.

15. The coaster will be very hot, so you should leave it to get cool before you touch it. When it is cool, you can peel the design off of it.

Customized doormat

Materials needed

- Cricut machine.

- Scrap cardstock (The color does not matter).

- Coir mat (18" x 30").

- Outdoor acrylic paint.

- Vinyl stencil.

- Transfer tape.

- Flat round paintbrush.

- Cutting mat (12" x 24").

Steps

1. Create your design in Cricut Design Space. You can also download an SVG design of your choice and import it into Cricut Design Space. Make sure that your design is the right size; resize it to ensure that this is so.

2. Next, you are to cut the stencil. You do this by clicking Make it in Cricut Design Space when you are done with the design. After this, you select Cardstock as the material. Then, you press the Cut button on the Cricut machine.

3. When this is done, remove the stencil from the machine and weed.

4. Next, on the reverse side of the stencil, apply spray glue. After this, attach the stencil to the doormat, exactly where you want your design to be; then, pick up the letter bits left on the cutting mat, and glue them to their places in the stencil on the doormat.

5. The next step is to mask the parts of the doormat which you do not want to paint on. You can do this using painter´s plastic.

6. Now, it's time to spray-paint your stencil on the doormat. Keeping the paint about 5 inches away from the doormat, spray up and down, keeping the can pointing straight through the stencil. If it is at an angle, the paint will get

under the stencil and ruin your design. Spray the entire stencil 2-3 times to make sure that you do not miss any part and that the paint is even.

7. You're just about done! Now, remove the masking plastic and the stencil and leave the doormat for about one hour to get dry.

T-Shirts (Vinyl, Iron On)

To make custom t-shirts using your Cricut machine, you will need to use iron-on or heat transfer vinyl. Ensure that you choose a color that contrasts and matches well with your t-shirt.

Materials needed

- Cricut machine.

- T-shirt.

- Iron on or heat transfer vinyl.

- Fine point blade and light grip mat.

- Weeding tools.

- Easy Press (regular household iron works fine too, with a little extra work).

- Small towel and Parchment paper.

Chapter 4 Advanced Tips And Techniques

The design Canvas platform

The following are ways you can work smarter on the design Canvas platform:

1. **Making use of cartridges for searching similar images:** Most times, the numerous outcomes of images gotten from the search bar in the image library can overwhelm a Cricut user. Whenever an image is searched, too many dissimilar results pop up. It, most of the time, makes it difficult to single out one favorite image out of these results. And sometimes, when a favorite image is found, more similar images are always wanted. To stop this from happening again, ensure that you make use of the cartridge of the image you're searching for. The easiest and fastest means of accessing a cartridge of an image is by clicking the small information (i) icon that is located at the bottom right of the image on the Design Space image library. By doing that, the image's details will be revealed. A green link will also appear, giving you access to every image

of equal similarity. Knowing this will enable you to start matching or coordinating images, which is more effective than the outcomes from the search bar.

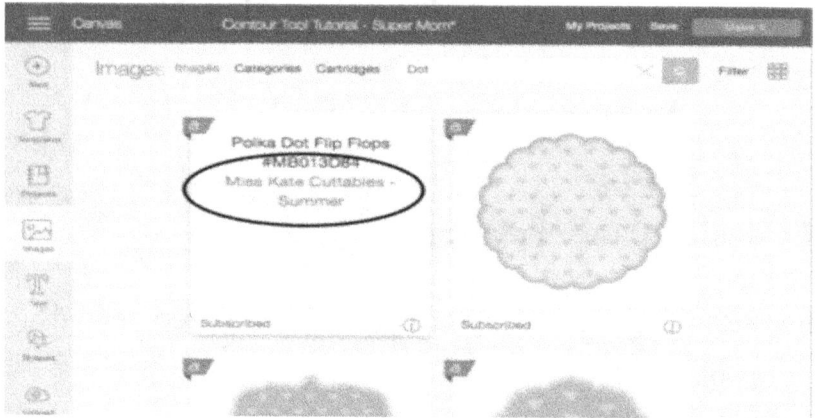

Photo credit- cricut.com

2. **Cutting, Drawing, or Scoring Lines:** In the past, Cricut users had to search for designs that had specific attributes for drawing and scoring a line (instead of cutting.) Not anymore, those days are behind all Cricut users. With the latest upgrade that has been made by Cricut on the Design Space, a user can comfortably change lines from cutting to drawing to scoring by merely making use of the easy-to-use Line type menu positioned at the topmost toolbar.

If you observe closely, you'll discover that almost all designs are tagged as Cut on the Design Space Canvas. Nonetheless, you can easily modify the outline of the image to be either scored (by utilizing the scoring wheel or) or drawn (by using pens.) All you need to do is to make sure that the layers of your design are ungrouped and unattached so that the way the project design will be created will change.

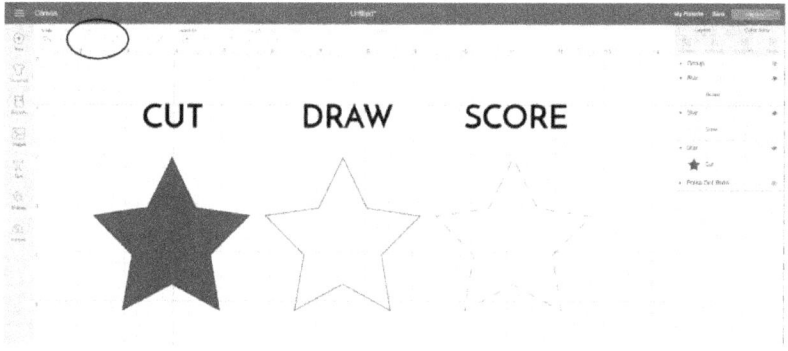

Photo credit- cricut.com

3. **Color Management:** If you can maximize the use of the Color Synchronization tool, you can significantly save much time working on different projects. This will likely ensure that you are using colors that match across various designs. A lot of times, when you work on a lot of designs on the design Canvas simultaneously, you may end up with several shades of similar colors. Instead of choosing all the single layers autonomously to recolor, go to the Color Sync tool positioned on the tool panel on the right side. The colors you will find on this panel are the ones that are presently in use. Notwithstanding, you can also drag active layers that are currently on the design by using your mouse and dropping it in a new color that hasn't been used on the design. If you desire to maintain the use of matching colors throughout your project designs, or you wish to have some layers with the same

color in order to cut more efficiently, making use of the Color Sync is the fastest and most comfortable means of doing it.

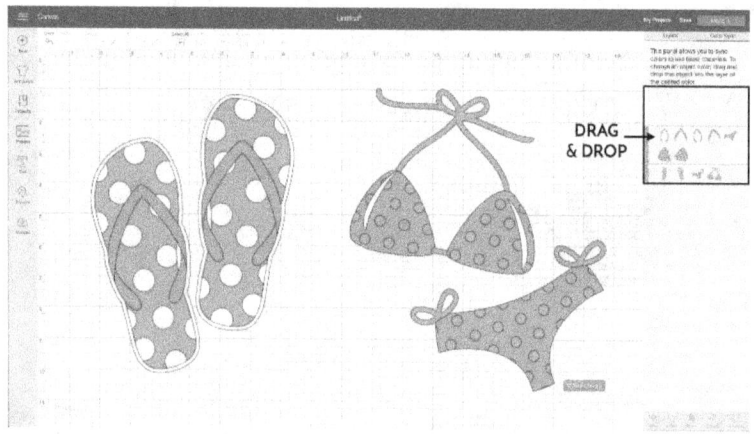

Photo credit- thehomesihavemade.com

4. **Applying the Hide tool:** A lot of users find themselves crowding the Canvas area with too many redundant images while they work on their projects. And they end up cutting all the elements on the Canvas area when the time comes to cut out their projects. There're likewise some times when you will wish or have to cut out some portions of the design you're working on. Instead of getting these unnecessary images deleted off your Canvas screen, you can just hide them by clicking the little eye icon positioned by the right side of the layers panel beside the image. You should note that any image you hide won't be permanently disconnected from the Canvas. However, it will not be added with the rest of the images when moving your project for cutting. You may also toggle the Hide icon on/off. This will make it easier to cut the parts needed only, and also keep an organized and clean design Canvas at

the same time, without getting the images you still want to work on mixed up.

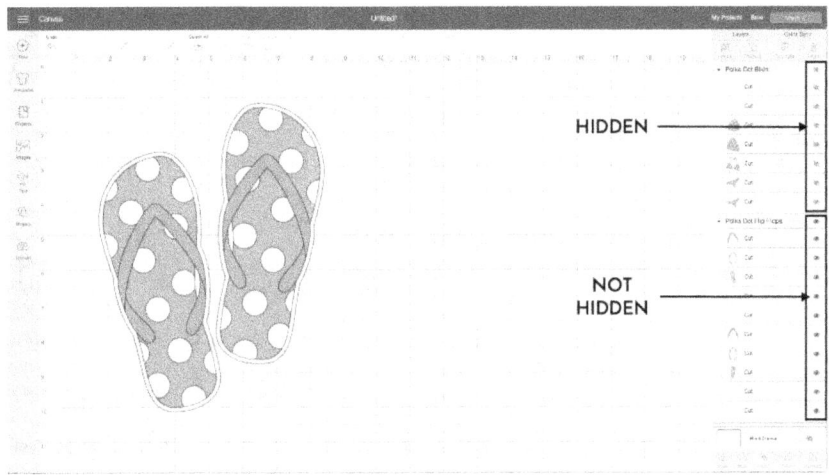

Photo credit- thehomesihavemade.com

5. **Adjust Image Patterns:** The Fill tool located at the topmost toolbar allows you to modify the way you fill images. Picking a single layer from the panel, colors can be switched, or the image interior can be given a different pattern.

There're quite a lot of pre-loaded patterns that can be used to fill images so as to make the project more stimulating without having to depend on patterned scrapbook or cardstock. Even though there're numerous designs to choose from, the scale and orientation of the chosen pattern can also be altered by clicking Edit Pattern located in the Pattern menu under the Fill panel. It is important to note that you can only use this function through the Print then cut method.

6. **Utilizing Keyboard Shortcuts:** Almost every computer program has keyboard shortcuts. Microsoft, Adobe, CorelDraw, and so on, they all have keyboard shortcuts. And just like them, the Design Space has keyboard shortcuts too. There are shortcuts for virtually every command you can think of, shortcuts for Copy, Cut, Paste, Duplicate, Undo, Delete, and many more. These functions are at the corner of every image, positioned at the topmost toolbar by the right side of the Layers panel. A lot of time can be saved by using as many shortcuts as possible. You can even try making use of functional keyboard shortcuts that work on other computer software out there. Most of these keyboard shortcuts are common; you can make use of Ctrl+C for copying, Ctrl+X for cutting, Ctrl+V for pasting, Ctrl+Z to undo mistakes, etc.

The Cut screen platform

A lot of Cricut users tend to think they won't be able to go further with their project editing once they send it for cutting after designing. They believe the editing ends immediately after clicking on the Make it button. But there are still so many actions and editing that a user can carry out on the Cut screen platform. And if done wisely, you will be able to save a lot of time and spare some materials.

1. **Moving mages around a single mat:** Even though the Design Space software automatically brings all your images

and designs on the surface of the mat according to color and orientation, it, most times, does not arrange them exactly the way you would want them. Nevertheless, these items can be moved around the mat surface while you're still on the Cut screen.

To reorganize your items on the mat surface, you can just start dragging and dropping the images where you need them to be. If you want, you can also rearrange by moving and rotating a cut however you want them on the mat. You can rotate the images by using the handles at the uppermost right corner of the Cut screen.

By making these adjustments, you won't only be able to make your work more perfect than the default settings would make it, you will also have your cut wherever and however you desire it. Your project looks better with these adjustments, especially when you're working on a scrap or an oddly-shaped material. Just make sure that your Cut screen gridlines are fit into the gridlines of your mat to ensure that your design fits the material correctly wherever it is placed.

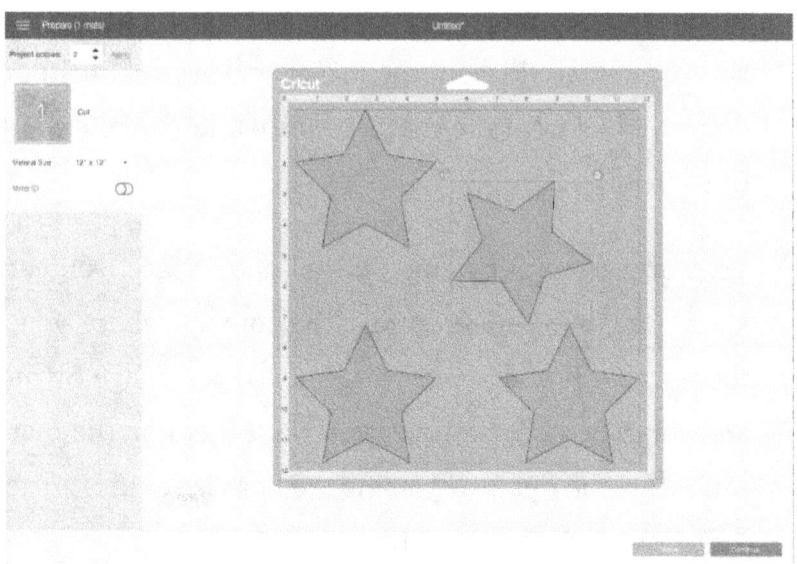

Photo credit- thehomesihavemade.com

2. **Moving images from a mat to another:** Although your images can be moved around just a single mat, you can likewise move the images from a mat to another without having to go back to the design Canvas to change colors. This can be done by clicking the three tiny dots positioned at the uppermost left side corner of that image you're currently working on. Once you've done that, select the Move to Another Mat option. Then you will be allowed to choose the mat you want that image to be on. You'll easily notice the change.

Photo credit- thehomesihavemade.com

This feature can be used anytime to conserve materials. If you're skillful enough, you can arrange all your images to fit into a single mat. This is also a perfect way of quickly changing the colors on designs without having to exit the Cut screen to manually modify the color of the designs.

3. **Re-cut or Skip Mats:** This feature will really prove useful to you if you just know how to use it on the Cut screen. After sending your designs for cutting, the remaining processes don't require much attention. As long as your Cricut machine is fed with the correct paper color and size just exactly as the Cut screen illustrates it, you shouldn't worry about the results; your project should come out precisely the way you designed it. Nonetheless, you may find yourself wanting to re-cut a particular mat after cutting it the first time or wishing to skip the mat that is next in line. The good

news is, that can be done easily without you needing to exit the Cut screen.

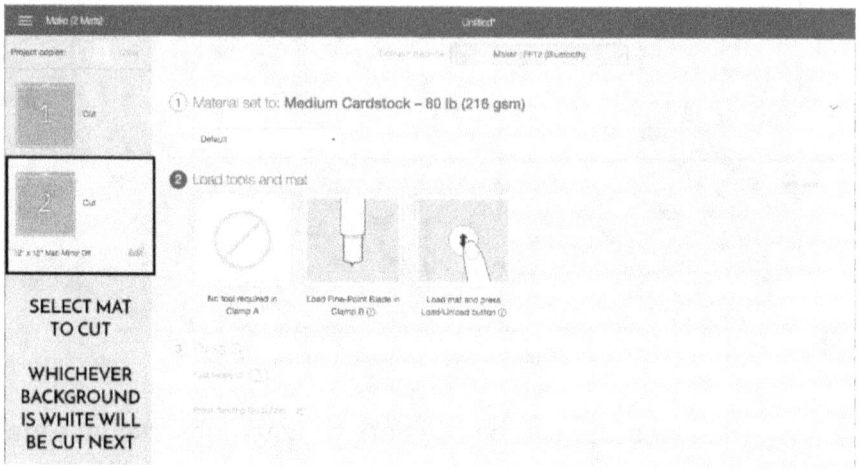

Photo credit- thehomesihavemade.com

However, you need to do this before you load your mat into the machine. You're free to select a particular mat you wish to cut manually by merely clicking or selecting the mat by the left-hand side of the Cut screen. The mat you handpicked will be skipped automatically by the cutting machine.

Moreover, if there is a particular mat you would like to re-cut, even after there're cut-marks all over it showing that the mat has been worked on already, return to the Cut screen and select that particular mat you want to manually re-cut. The Cricut machine will handle the rest automatically. However, much care must be taken when you re-cut or skip mats. Ensure you always double-check if what you're loading into the machine fits perfectly into the emphasized mat on the Cut Screen. A lot of Cricut users make mistakes so many times whenever they re-cut or skip mats without full attention.

4. **Saving commonly used materials:** Many Cricut users feel stunned always when they learn about this particular feature after using the Cricut software for a long time. They realized how much they'd missed! You're certainly missing so much if you're not making use of the Custom materials option. A lot of people, especially those people making use of the Explore Air 2 series, do not make use of this feature unintentionally because their Cricut machine is set to Vinyl, Iron-in, Cardstock, etc. Only people that use the Cricut Maker machine can notice the Custom materials function within the Design Space easily since there is no available option to choose the material you are cutting.

Photo credit- cricut.com

You don't have to go through the stress of strolling through more than a hundred custom materials so as to find the common Cardstock, Vinyl, and Iron-on Vinyl settings over and over again. You can just add each one of these to the Favorite box. It shouldn't take you more than a few minutes to stroll through the Materials menu and locate the materials that you make use of regularly. Just click on the star positioned under the Materials menu, and then proceed to select Favorites instead of Popular on that same menu. Once you've done that, all that will be left is just a menu showing all the materials you mostly cut. That is way easier and comfortable, right?

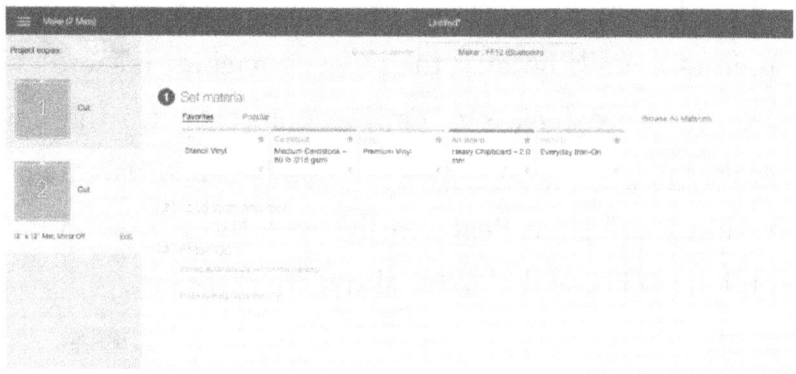

Photo credit- cricut.com

5. **Connecting Two or More Cricut Machines Simultaneously:** Even though a typical Cricut user doesn't often make use of more than a single Cricut machine, it's possible to connect more than one machine to your Design Space account at the same time. You can do this by either using Bluetooth when using a wireless machine model or using a USB with your PC. Moreover, you

shouldn't worry about getting your machines and your designs mixed up during the cutting session. The number of Cricut machines you connect to your Design Space doesn't matter. The first step you'll take when you reach the Cut screen is to select which machine you want to use to cut your design. You will find this function in a drop-down menu located at the top. With this step, Cricut ensures that its users can stay assured that they're using the intended machine for their project all the time.

6. **Easily Adjusting Cut Pressure:** Even though it looks fantastic to have the capability of modifying your materials' settings, sometimes all that is required is an extra or lesser pressure to allow your Cricut machine to efficiently cut through the material you set. If you want to adjust the cut pressure, once you've selected your material of choice on the Cut screen, adjust the pressure by using the drop-down menu provided at the top. You can choose to decrease, increase, or make use of the default pressure. Using this technique, you can effortlessly and swiftly change your cutting depth without having to rummage around the custom settings of your material.

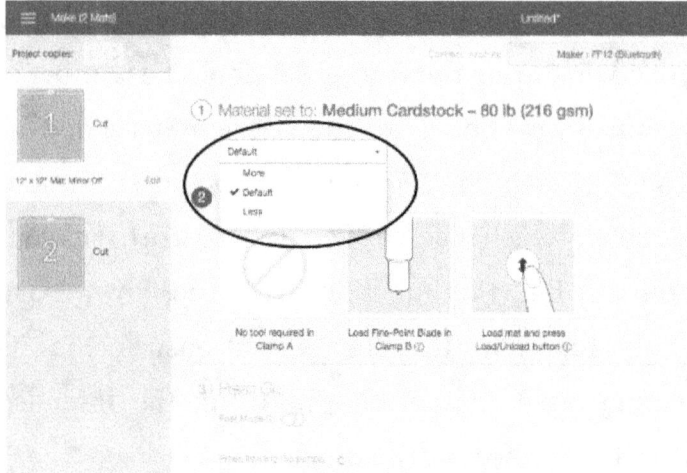

Photo credit- cricut.com

7. **Mirror Setting:** There're times when Cricut users have to do their design cutting in reverse, particularly when they are working on projects with Iron-on. This process of reversing is known as Mirror. Although your designs can always be flipped on the Canvas screen horizontally, there is also an option provided to mirror designs while using the Cut screen.

This setting doesn't only enable you to mirror the images or mats you want to flip; it also allows you to create and adjust your designs without having to flip them on the Canvas screen. It gets easier to view and customize your designs on the mat.

Photo credit- thehomesihavemade.com

8. **Filling your mat by adjusting project copies**: A lot of Cricut users don't get to use this cool Auto-fill function, either by unawareness or unavailability. This function can only be accessed on Cricut machine models that are old. Using the old machine models, a single star can be put on your Canvas, and you can select your paper size manually, and then select Auto-fill without stress. Once you click on Auto-fill, your Cricut machine will fill up the paper with stars automatically, fitting in as many stars as your paper can comfortably take. Even though you will not find this function in the most recent Design Space, there is an easy way of doing almost the same thing the function does.

There is a particular option located at the uppermost part of the Cut screen once you reach the Cut screen platform where the settings of your project copies can be done. This function allows you to cut for as much time as you want on the Design Canvas. Although it could take some time to figure out the exact number of project copies you need to fill your mat, it's way faster than duplicating your designs on the Design Canvas.

All the tips and techniques that have been given so far should be carefully studied. Some of them may look subtle, but you shouldn't overlook them if you don't want to end up wasting your time or materials. Many full-time Cricut users are always on the hunt for information on how they can save time and materials while on the Design Space. The information is in your hand right now, what you do with it is now your decision.

Using advanced design space tools

There are some many Design Space tools that will look mysterious to a beginner or new user. Some will almost seem meaningless and redundant. However, these tools are not useless or worthless; you just don't know how to make use of them yet. The following are some of the advanced tools on the Design Space.

The Flatten tool

The Flatten tool has a lot of usefulness. It's not just a tool that flattens; it performs more than one function. Below are some of its functions:

- The Flatten tool changes multi-layered pictures into one single-layered image.

- It is used to convert an image to a printable image, to enable it for print-and-cut.

- It removes every cut line from an image.

- It retains every color of a multi-layered image.

How to make use of the Flatten tool

- Pick the layers that you want to flatten by clicking on Select All, or by pressing and holding the Ctrl key on the keyboard while clicking on the layers.

- When you've selected all the layers you want, click on Flatten positioned at the lower right corner.

- Once you've done that, your image becomes flattened. All you will see on the Layers panel is one layer with a text that says, Flatten.

The Color Sync tool

Like the Flatten tool, the Color Sync tool also has more than one function for Design Space users who know their way around it. Below are some of its functions:

- The Color Sync tool can be used to recolor shapes, layers, etc.

- It can be used to match the colors of all layers on the Canvas.

- It is very useful for consolidating material colors.

- It saves a user so much time and materials.

This feature wasn't available in the old version of the Design Space. But now that it is available in the new version, why not make exploits with it? This tool makes it much more comfortable to synchronize colors in a project so a user can cut them all on a single material. All you have to do is open the Color Sync panel located at the right side of the screen, and then start dragging and dropping all the shapes respectively into the selected layer you wish for it to synchronize to. If you desire to cut every star in chartreuse, for example, then just drag every other star to that same layer at the Color Sync panel. It feels so much easier to do this, and knowing they are all going to have the same color is comforting!

Sketching on the Design Space

One of the most interesting facts about using the Cricut Explore model is that users can also upload images that they have drawn themselves! There are two techniques of doing this, one is by making use of Illustrator, and the other is by making use of the Design Space. And since we're discussing about the Design Space,

I'll only mention how to do so on the latter. The following are the processes:

- You first need to have the intended image on your computer by importing it. So, if you've hand-drawn what you want on a piece of paper or your tablet, the next step is to scan it to your computer, snap it with your mobile device and send it to your computer, or save and send it to the computer through your tablet. Whichever way you want to do it, ensure you save it as a png or jpeg file.

- Convert the sketch using the Design Space by first uploading the image, making use of the Upload tab by the left side.

- You will be requested to choose the image type; you should select the option that fits your image background. Proceed by clicking Continue and let your image be saved as a Cut image, and then click Save. You will notice that your image is now a Cut file.

And that's how you upload and work with your sketch on the Design Space. With this function, you can let your creativity run wild! There are so many things you can do with your hands! Since you're not limited by the Design Space platform, don't ever let your imagination be limited!

Chapter 5 Other Tips & Tricks

There are so many tricks that can help you use your Cricut machine better and faster to ensure that you are getting the most out of it.

Each machine has tips and tricks to make it work better. We tell you what sites you can go on and what stores you can go to find supplies as well. Many people assume that the only place that you can go to get this kind of supplies is a crafting store. A crafting store is one of the best places that you can get the supplies because they do offer discounts in certain cases and they offer great quality for the products you want. However, they are not the only store that gives high-quality products, and we'll let you know where you can go and to get supplies of high-quality but do not cost an arm and a leg. People do not know that you can go into other stores because the craft world can come with a stigma that you are supposed to shop only in crafting stores. This is not true, however, and we will tell you how to get great supplies.

We give you tips on how to clean your machine and what not to do which is going to help you to be able to understand just how easy it is to damage your machine. These machines can be very temperamental and doing the wrong thing can damage them in a way that makes it so you might have to buy another machine. As these machines are a hefty investment, you do not want to break it on accident, and we have given you tips for how to avoid this.

There are also tips on things you can use instead of the supplies that are listed here. Meaning, if you are in a pinch and you run out of your regular supplies, there are things that you can use instead. We also give you some great tips on how to get the best quality of work from your machine and how to keep your machine running at its best. This is going to be great for you as an owner because this means that you are going to be able to make your machine last longer. For the people that do not have information about their machine, and they do not know how to take care of their machine, their machine is going to wear out much quicker. So, let us dive into our tips and tricks!

- Look in other places besides craft stores to find supplies. Some great examples are sites like eBay or look into clearance sales. One of the best places that people have found to be a great place for supplies is 'Dollar Tree'. You can find vinyl, fabric, or boards to use.

- Another tip that ties into the Dollar Tree is that you can find supplies for transforming your craft room into how you want it and finding tools to keep your supplies organized.

- Curling is a big problem with projects, and this next tip is going to show you how you can avoid it by remembering not to peel the paper away from your cutting mat. Peel the cutting mat away from the paper instead. Roll your mat backward away from the material that you're cutting. This is especially true if you are cutting paper. If you do this, you will get a nice cut and flat project. If you do not do this, then it can curl massively and shred along with tearing.

- Keeping your mats clean is also going to be a great way to make them last longer so you do not have to replace them as often and waste your money. A great tip for keeping those mats clean is to use your lint roller. Make sure that you have removed all the little papers and roll away. The lint roller trick is especially beneficial if you have been cutting glitter cardstock. Since this does not remove everything, you should be aware of that, but it will get rid of most things.

- Freezer paper makes great stencils and you can get it for only a dollar!

- Keeping your blades separate and organized will help too. Having separate blades for vinyl or fabric will help the blades stay sharp and the way you need them to longer. Keeping the blades separate is also going to help you be more organized. If you want, you can use a permanent marker on each of the blades so that you know what blade is for what particular material you want to cut with them. It is like owning a pair of fabric scissors. You would not use fabric scissors to cut paper, so instead, keep your blades sharp by keeping them separate. You can make a small mark which blades are for what material. If you do not want to use the marker on them, you can make a chart. Just remember to replace the cap so that they are not getting mixed up.

- You can also spray paint on your vinyl if you need color and don't have it, just make sure it's a Rust-oleum metallic spray and give it a quick spray. Make sure the vinyl isn't cut and dry it before cutting. This is going to help ensure that you have the proper cutting techniques and you have the proper settings in place. This also ensures that you are not wasting materials, time or money.

- Besides Cricut pens, there are a variety of other options that work for Explore machines. They include American Crafts, Recollection, Sharpies, or even Crayola.

- You can also use your system fonts in your projects. You can go to sites that offer fonts to find a lot of amazing ones for free and then you can use them for your machine.

- If you have a smaller or more intricate design you can use a weeding box. This is especially helpful if you're cutting multiple designs on one mat.

- Make sure that your dial is set to the correct setting for materials. It is very easy to forget that this is in the wrong setting and then the cut can be wrong.

- Load your mat correctly. Both sides of the mat need to be able to slide under the rollers or the mat will not cut in the correct manner.

- When you can no longer make a smooth cut or an effective cut, you need new blades. Be careful when replacing them because you can cut yourself pretty badly.

- You can clean your cutting mats with baby wipes as well. They need to be water-based and using them to keep your mats clean can help them stay sticky longer. Make sure that these baby wipes have no fragrance. If they are not water-based, they will damage the mat and you will not be able to use it again.

- Keep the plastic sheets that come with your mats and you can protect the mats between uses. This helps your mats last longer so that you can use them repeatedly.

- If you are not sure about the correct cut setting, run a small test cut first. This is especially true if you have a larger project. Doing this is going to make sure that you are not wasting expensive materials that you want and need. It will also make sure you understand what cuts can do to materials.

- Your vinyl needs to be placed the right way up on the cutting mat. The heat transfer vinyl should always be placed shiny side down.

- When you are cutting heat transfer vinyl, you need to remember to mirror the design. This is crucial because if you do not, then you will be cutting incorrectly, and your project could be ruined as a result.

- The Cricut toolset is not a necessity, but it can certainly help, and it can be a great thing to have on hand when you're mastering your machine. It also has many different items that can make your crafting easier and less of a hassle.

- Many card projects require that you have a stylus. If the machine you bought is part of a bundle it can have the stylus inside it already, but some may not. This is something to ask the person at the store when you are buying one because the stylus can really help.

- Make sure that you do a practice project before a real one as well because this will let you get adjusted to your machine and make sure that you do not waste materials on your first project. When you buy your machine, there should be a practice project already in place.

- Make sure that your blade is placed correctly. If it is placed too high, it may only cut part of the way through, but if it is down to low, it will ruin your mat. A test cut will make sure it is in the right spot therefore could save you a lot of frustration.

- Many people forget that the pen is in their machine after finishing a project and that can be a big no-no. The reason for this is because if the lid is not on it, it will dry out and the pens can get very expensive. So be sure to put the pen cap back on and make sure it is all the way on.

- Keeping some supplies on demand is a good idea as well, particularly if you're going to be working with vinyl and cardstock. Since most projects use vinyl, you could have some of that on hand along with a pack of cardstock and things of that nature.

- Know which machine has which options on it. The machines are different and can come with different settings as well.

- When your mat loses its stickiness, you may think that you have to buy a new one. You do not, however, at least in most cases, because there are tips you can use here too. Clean your mat and see if that works and then tape your project down to hold it in place. Not over an area that needs to be cut but just over a few edges. A tack paint that is medium tape is good for this and shouldn't damage the cardstock.

- A trick for installing fonts into your computer, you may need to sign out of the app and then back in before your new font will show up. If this does not work, then be sure to restart your computer.

- The deep cut blade is a handy tip here as well. Having the deep blade means you can cut through thicker materials like chipboard, felt, and leather. It is compatible with the Explore Air 2. Just make sure when you get this blade, you get the housing for it as well.

- If you have a project that cuts on two different materials (such as a pink cardstock and a purple cardstock), you can do this at the same time by positioning the designs you will be cutting in different areas of the Canvas on your app. Click Attach, then position the materials in the same spot on the map. This tip can be applied to Design Space for desktop and web.

If you use all of these tips, you will be able to use your machine to your heart's content and make any project. You will also be able to save money so that you're not spending a fortune on supplies every time you run out. Utilize these to your benefit and enjoy being able to use your machine with better knowledge.

Chapter 6 Common Problems And How To Solve Them

Material tearing or not cutting completely through

This is the biggest problem with most Cricut users. When this happens, the image is ruined, and you've wasted material. More machines have been returned or boxed up and put away due to this problem than any other.

But don't panic, if your paper is not cutting correctly there are several steps you can take to try and correct the problem.

Most important is this: Anytime you work with the blade TURN YOUR MACHINE OFF. I know it's easy to forget this because you're frustrated and you're trying this and that to make it work correctly. But this is an important safety precaution that you should remember.

Make simple adjustments at first. Turn the pressure down one. Did it help? If not, turn the blade down one number. Also, make sure the mat is free of debris so the blade rides smoothly.

Usually the thicker the material, the higher the pressure number should be set to cut through the paper. Don't forget to use the multi-cut function if you have that option. It may take a little longer to cut 2, 3, or 4 times, but by then it should cut clean through.

For those of you using the smaller bugs that do not have that option here is how to make your multi-cut function. After the image has been cut, don't unload the mat just hit load paper, repeat last, and cut. You can repeat this sequence 2, 3, or 4 times to ensure your image is completely cut out.

If you are using thinner paper and it is tearing try reducing the pressure and slowing down the speed. When cutting intricate designs, you have to give the blade enough time to maneuver through the design. By slowing it down it will be able to make cleaner cuts.

Clean the edge of the blade to be sure no fuzz, glue, or scraps of paper are stuck to it.

Make sure the blade is installed correctly. Take it out and put it back so it's seated firmly. The blade should be steady while it's making cuts. If it makes a shaky movement it's either not installed correctly, or there's a problem with the blade housing.

Be aware that there is a deep cutting blade for thicker material. You'll want to switch to this blade when you're cutting heavy card stock. This will also save wear and tear on your regular blade. Cutting a lot of thick material will wear your blade out quicker than thinner material and cause you to change it more often.

Machine freezing

Remember to always turn your machine off when you switch cartridges. When you switch cartridges leaving the machine on it's called "hot swapping" and it can sometimes cause the machine to freeze. This is more of an issue with the older models and doesn't seem to apply to the Expression 2.

You know how peculiar electronic gadgets can be, so give your machine a rest for five or ten minutes every hour. If you work for several hours continuously, your machine might overheat and freeze up.

Turn the machine off and take a break. Restart it when you come back and it should be fine. Then remember not to rush programming the machine and give it an occasional rest.

Don't press a long list of commands quickly. If you give it too much information too quickly it will get confused in the same way a computer sometimes does and simply freeze up. Instead of typing in one long phrase try dividing up your words into several cuts.

If you're using special feature keys make sure you press them first before selecting the letters.

Power problems

If you turn your machine on and nothing happens the power adapter may be at fault. Jiggle the power cord at the outlet and where it connects to the machine to make sure it's firmly connected. Ideally, you want to test the adapter before buying a new one. Swap cords with a friend and see if that fixed the problem. Replacement adapters can be found on eBay by searching for a Cricut adapter power supply.

The connection points inside the machine may also pose a problem; here is how to test that. Hold down the plug where it inserts into the back of the machine and turn it on. If it powers up, then the problem is inside the machine and the connection points will have to be soldered again.

If the machine powers up but will not cut then try a hard reset. See the resource section for step-by-step instructions on resetting your machine.

Here are a few tips especially for Expression 2 users. Have you turned on your machine, you watch it light up and hear it gearing up but when you try to cut nothing happens? Or you're stuck on the welcome screen or the LCD screen is unresponsive.

Well here are two quick fixes to try. First, try a hard reset sometimes called the rainbow screen reset to recalibrate your die cutter. If that does not resolve the problem you're going to have to restore the settings.

To help cut down on errors try to keep your machine updated. When an update is available, you should receive a message encouraging you to install the latest version.

For those of you using third-party software that is no longer compatible with the Cricut you probably already know that updating your machine may disable that software.

When you cut heavy paper and your Expression 2 shuts down try switching to the normal paper setting and use the multi-cut function.

Carriage will not move

If the carriage assembly does not move, check to see if the belt has broken or if the car has fallen off the track. Provo Craft does not sell replacement parts, which is nuts, so try to find a compatible belt at a vacuum repair shop.

If the wheels have fallen off the track, remove the plastic cover, and look for a tiny screw by the wheel unscrew it. You now should be able to move the wheel back on track.

Unresponsive keyboard

If you are sure you are pressing the keys firmly, you have a cartridge inserted correctly and a mat loaded ready to go, but the keypad is still not accepting your selection, the problem may be internal.

You will have to remove the keyboard and check if the display cable is connected to the keypad and to the motherboard. If the connections are secure then you have a circuit board problem and repairs are beyond the scope of this book.

An important reminder, please do not attempt any repairs unless your machine is out of warranty.

Weird LCD screen

The LCD screen is now showing strange symbols or is blank after doing a firmware update. Try running the update again making sure your selections are correct.

When the image you choose is bigger than the mat or paper size you selected, the preview screen will look grayed out instead of showing the image. So, increase the paper and mat size or decrease the size of your image.

Also, watch out for the gray box effect when using the center point feature. Move the start position down until you see the image appear. The same thing may happen when using the fit to length feature. Try changing to landscape mode and shorten the length size until the image appears.

Occasionally using the undo button will cause the preview screen to turn black; unfortunately, the only thing to do is turn the machine off. Your work will be lost and you have to start again.

Cartridge errors

Sometimes dust or debris accumulates in the cartridge port; gently blow out any paper fiber that may have collected in the opening. Make sure the contact points are clean and that nothing is preventing the cartridge from being read properly.

With any electrical machine overheating can be a problem. If you get a cartridge error after using your machine for a while turn it off and let it cool down for about fifteen minutes.

If this is the very first time you're using the cartridge and you get an error I'm sure you know the trick about turning the cartridge around and inserting it in backward.

If you thought you could use your Imagine cartridges with your Expression 2, think again. You will get an error message because you can only use the art cartridges that you can cut with, the colors and patterns cartridges are for printing.

Even brand-new items fresh out of the box can be defective. If you see a cartridge error 1, 2, 3, 4, 5, 6, 9, or 99 call customer service and tell them the name, serial number, and error message number and they may replace the cartridge.

Trouble connecting to your computer

All Cricut machines come with a USB cord that lets you connect to your computer and allows you to use the other products like the Cricut Design Studio software, Cricut Craft Room, or the Cricut Gypsy with your machines.

Double check your USB connection and try another port.

Check to see if you may have a firewall or antivirus software that is blocking the connection.

See if you're running the latest firmware. You may need to update. Older machines update via firmware (Personal Cutter, Expression, Create, and Cake) the newer (Expression 2, Imagine, and Gypsy) use the Sync program to update.

When anything else fails

I know that no one wants to hear this. But there are going to be times when you may have to resort to calling customer service. This is especially true if your machine is still under warranty. You don't' want to do anything that might void the warranty on a truly defective machine.

Sadly, Prove Craft is known for its long wait times and sometimes less than stellar service. Stick it out and demand that your machine is fixed or replaced.

After a while, you may notice some of your projects coming out in a condition that is less-than-crisp.

Ensure your machine is on stable footing

This may seem pretty basic but ensuring that your machine is on a level surface will allow it to make more precise cuts every single time. Rocking of the machine or wobbling could cause unstable results in your projects.

Ensure no debris has gotten stuck under the feet of your machine that could cause instability before proceeding to the next troubleshooting step!

Redo all cable connections

So, your connections are in the best possible working order, undo all your cable connections, blow into the ports or use canned air, and then securely plug everything back into the right ports. This will help to make sure all the connections are talking to each other where they should be!

Completely dust and clean your machine

Your little Cricut works hard for you! Return the favor by making sure you're not allowing gunk, dust, grime, or debris to build up in the surfaces and crevices. Adhesive can build up on the machine around the mat input and on the rollers, so be sure to focus on those areas!

Check your blade housing

Sometimes debris and leavings from your materials can build up inside the housings for your blades! Open them up and clear any built-up materials that could be impeding swiveling or motion.

Sharpen your blades

A very popular Cricut trick in use is to stick a clean, fresh piece of foil to your Cricut mat, and run it through with the blade you wish to sharpen. Running the blades through the thin metal helps to revitalize their edges and give them a little extra staying power until it's time to buy replacements.

Another way to do this is to make a ball of foil, remove the blades from the housing, and stick them into the ball of foil several times until you notice a shine on the blade. This can give you a better idea of how sharpened your blades are becoming before you finish up with them, and it seems like a more expedient way to sharpen several blades in one sitting, but the reviews seem to be equally as positive as letting your machine do the work for you on one blade at a time.

Conclusion

The following step is to utilize your new found wisdom on the cutting edge craft project designing and creation offered by "Cricut". You are now poised to follow the detailed instructions described in this manuscript to create your own personalized and one of a kind craft projects that reflect your creativity and serve as an exhibit of your expression.

The possibilities that the Cricut machine has to offer are endless. Every craftsman, beginner, or professional creates beautiful craft pieces according to their level of expertise regarding the Cricut Machine, and after reading this manuscript, you will not be left out. This manuscript has deliberated enough information that you are already ready to go and perform a great artwork of which the world will be proud. So get to work straight away and start creating beautiful crafts. Owning this type of machine is a prime opportunity for many people to develop their expertise in craftsmanship, and it's incredible if you want to venture out and try new things as a crafter because you can add so many new items to your portfolio.

As a result, this machine can literally offer never-ending opportunities for a crafter.

In this manuscript, we've discussed how to set up your Cricut machine as well as the advantages of owning one, and we gave you all the information you need to be able to use it efficiently and effectively. It is very typical to get overwhelmed when you own a Cricut machine because of all the information. Still, we told you exactly what you need to know to get started and start creating impressive and innovative projects. There's so much information out there, and the best part is that most of it is free, which means you have more opportunities to get images and things you need to craft, but it also means you get a much bigger chance to get ideas for your projects.

Most people don't even know where to get information about their machine or the items they can use to start crafting, but this manuscript has all the information you need from describing the Cricut machine's most basic function to reflecting ideas for experienced users. We have also shown you that once you have the required skills and the right resources, you can cut even more with the Cricut machines, so you are aware of this as well. In this way, we've made sure you can never forget exactly what you can cut using this machine. However, if you're ever confused, there's a whole part in this manuscript on how to set up your machine and how to set up your design space. We have also included some helpful hints and tips to make sure you have some great ideas on how to make it easier for you to use this machine and the supplies, and you can use all of these tips to your advantage. If you follow the tips you've found in this manuscript, you're going to be able to find supplies easier, keep your mats cleaner, use your machine way better, maintain your machine considerably better, and even gain some amazing storage tips and actually make your craft space a place you can be proud of and feel happy and content while you're working. The ability to do that will help boost both your craftsmanship and your emotions.

Cricut Design Space is a web-based program just as a partner application and now a beta Desktop software that permits you to make, transfer, and oversee records to work the Cricut Maker and Cricut Explore machines. You can get to the application remotely in individual machines, utilizing your PC, tablet, and even cell phone. Cricut Design Space™ additionally permits you to get to a library of tasks and files to download.

www.ingramcontent.com/pod-product-compliance
Lightning Source LLC
Chambersburg PA
CBHW071528080526
44588CB00011B/1594